The Divine Name

Also by Jonathan Goldman

Books
Healing Sounds
Shifting Frequencies
The Lost Chord
Tantra of Sound (with Andi Goldman)
*The 7 Secrets of Sound Healing**

Music CDs
Trance Tara
Sacred Gateways
Dolphins Dreams
Chakra Chants (vol. 1 and 2)
*The Divine Name** (with Gregg Braden)
Holy Harmony
Celestial Yoga
Reiki Chants
The Angel and the Goddess
The Lost Chord
De-Stress
Waves of Light
Celestial Reiki (vol. 1, with Laraaji; vol. 2, with Laraaji and Sarah Benson)
Frequencies
ChakraDance
Medicine Buddha
Ultimate Om
2012: Ascension Harmonics
2013: Ecstatic Sonics
Waves of Light
Crystal Bowls Chakra Chants (with Crystal Tones)

Instructional CDs
Healing Sounds Instructional
Vocal Toning the Chakras

DVD
Healing Sounds

*Available from Hay House

Please visit:
Hay House USA: **www.hayhouse.com**®
Hay House Australia: **www.hayhouse.com.au** • Hay House UK: **www.hayhouse.co.uk**
Hay House South Africa: **www.hayhouse.co.za** • Hay House India: **www.hayhouse.co.in**

The Divine Name

The Sound That Can Change the World

Jonathan Goldman

HAY HOUSE, INC.

Carlsbad, California • New York City
London • Sydney • Johannesburg
Vancouver • Hong Kong • New Delhi

Published and distributed in the United States by: Hay House, Inc.: www.hayhouse.com •
Published and distributed in Australia by: Hay House Australia Pty. Ltd.: www.hayhouse.
com.au • *Published and distributed in the United Kingdom by:* Hay House UK, Ltd.: www.
hayhouse.co.uk • *Published and distributed in the Republic of South Africa by:* Hay House SA
(Pty), Ltd.: www.hayhouse.co.za • *Distributed in Canada by:* Raincoast: www.raincoast.com
• *Published in India by:* Hay House Publishers India: www.hayhouse.co.in

Editorial supervision: Jill Kramer • *Project editor:* Alex Freemon • *Design:* Nick C. Welch

Grateful acknowledgment is made to Roger Nelson and the Global Consciousness Project,
http://noosphere.princeton.edu, for permission to reprint the chart on page 190; and to
Guy Coggins and Aura Imaging Systems, **www.auraphoto.com**, for permission to reprint
the photos on page 198.

Library of Congress Control Number: 2009926842

ISBN: 978-1-4019-2699-1

13 12 11 10   5 4 3 2
1st edition, March 2010
2nd edition, October 2010

Printed in the United States of America

FSC
Mixed Sources
Product group from well-managed
forests, controlled sources and
recycled wood or fiber
Cert no. BV-COC-930557
www.fsc.org
© 1996 Forest Stewardship Council

It is time to revive
My Name,
Lest it be forgotten.

Contents

Foreword

Three thousand five hundred years ago a shepherd walked away from the safety of his home and the love of his family to follow a calling that only he could hear. What he experienced, nearly a millennium and a half before the birth of Jesus, has become the source of the greatest divisions between nations, as well as the greatest unity between people; the reason for the darkest wars in history, as well as the strongest peace; the key to the deepest sense of belonging, and the most miraculous healings in history. The event that transpired on that day so long ago continues to shape our lives today.

Walking across the barren floor of the Egyptian desert, that lone pilgrim began a journey on behalf of all humans, past and present, not knowing when—or even if—he would ever return. His pilgrimage led him to an ancient and desolate mountaintop rising more than 7,000 feet above sea level. We can only wonder if he sensed that the ground under his feet would become one of the most sacred, and controversial, places on Earth.

The mountain was Sinai.

The man's name was Moses.

When he reached the mountaintop, Moses spoke with God.

And if such a conversation wasn't extraordinary enough, before he returned to those he left behind, Moses did the unthinkable. He asked God a question. But not just any question. He asked the one question that had to be asked if his experience was to be accepted by the people of his time—and remain meaningful to us today. Addressing the Deity that would later give him "the Law" of the Ten Commandments, Moses asked God to reveal His name! Today, three and a half millennia later, we're still talking about God's answer.

In what can only be described as one of the most profound, mysterious, and compassionate revelations of human history, God answered Moses with the actual sound of the heavenly code that had never been shared on Earth before that moment: the sound of His personal name—the Divine Name. And this is what makes

Moses's experience unique. Historical records suggest that he is the only one of us who has ever heard God's personal name spoken on Earth by God Himself. And just so there would be no doubt as to precisely what it was that he had heard, Moses was given a written record of his conversation with God—a hard copy containing the code by which we may know God in this world.

Contrary to some theories suggesting that Moses transcribed his conversation with the Divine, the scholarly translation of the oldest record of that moment, the Torah, states that "He [God] gave Moses the two tablets of the Pact, stone tablets inscribed with the finger of God" (Exodus 31:18). The implications of this single statement are profound. The assertion that the tablets were "inscribed with the finger of God" removes any doubt as to Who was doing the writing. The words came directly from Whoever or whatever God is.

Rather than the general names that biblical texts often use to describe the character or attributes of God, such as *El Elyon* (God Most High), *El Shaddai* (God Almighty), or *I Am,* God revealed a unique, direct, tangible, and very personal name through his gift to Moses. In Exodus 3:15, God describes the significance of what he has done, stating:

"This shall be My name forever,
This My appellation for all eternity."

For more than three millennia since that time, the Divine Name has been welcomed, protected, misused, worshipped, feared, celebrated, sung, intoned, chanted, and hidden from the masses. In later translations of the Torah, God's name was removed in 6,800 instances and replaced with substitute terms that were meant to identify the "unspeakable" name of God without stating it directly. Even today, the speaking or writing of the name revealed to Moses is prohibited in some Orthodox religious traditions. The question is: *why?* What is it about the ancient and personal name of God that could possibly hold such power that it warrants such strict rules and guidelines? The answer to that question is where this book, *The Divine Name,* comes in.

Throughout the many years I have known Jonathan Goldman as a colleague and friend, many of our weekly conversations have revolved around the topic of the Divine Name. Our friendship and deep reverence for the power of this ancient code became even deeper with the discovery that God's ancient name is encoded in the DNA of all life (see my book *The God Code,* Hay House, 2004) and the statistical proof that this discovery was beyond chance. It's intentional.

So now we must ask ourselves, what does it all mean? What does it mean to have the ancient name of God inscribed into the very core of the stuff we're made of? What is it about the ancient name of God that is so vital to our existence that Who, or what, placed it into our bodies long ago knew that the only way to preserve such a powerful message would be to encode it into the very life that it was intended for?

In the pages that follow, Jonathan brings his experience, heart, and hope for our future to a crystal clear, laser-clean focus in order to answer precisely these questions . . . and more. In a way that only he can do, Jonathan reveals how the Divine Name affects our bodies, relationships, and lives. And then he invites us to go one step further—he shares the ancient instructions for creating the sound of God's name in a way that honors the reason it has remained hidden for centuries.

- Knowing that the Divine Name lives within every one of us gives us the reason to *feel beyond* the differences that have separated us in the past.

- Sounding the Divine Name catapults us into the next level of acceptance, anchoring our feeling at the deepest levels of awareness.

This book is your key to doing both of the above. You can think of it as a condensed initiation into the great mystery schools of the past. It's your users' manual for inviting God's personal name into your life.

How will you use the power of the Divine Name to guide you through the uncharted territory of the great physical and spiritual crises of our time? That's the unwritten chapter of our history that is yours to complete. For more than 3,000 years, God's name has played a powerful role in leading us to healthier, happier, and more empowered lives. Today, as the experts tell us we face the greatest challenges in 5,000 years of recorded human history, why would we expect that the Divine Name would do any less for us?

— **Gregg Braden**
Taos, New Mexico

Introduction

$\mathcal{W}$e are living in extraordinary times—crucial eras of great shifts and transformation. Many believe that this is a period quite pivotal to our very survival on the planet and to the planet itself. It is of paramount importance that we as a species unite, and experience a quantum evolutionary leap in human consciousness. The question is: *how?*

What if you had discovered a form of technology that had the potential to unite the world and bring peace to the planet? What if you'd found a technique for sounding the personal name of God that could change the world? What would you do? This was my dilemma once I had made the discovery. It began with a dream and now unfolds in this book.

You hold in your hands a very powerful tool: a gateway . . . a bridge to another state of being. The technology it's based upon is of the heart. It's a key from the past that may unlock the door to the future. You'll discover and learn the power of the Divine Name—the lost sound of the personal name of God— and how to utilize it for healing and transformation. Through this practice, you'll gain the ability to bring balance and harmony to yourself and the planet.

This isn't a theoretical text, but rather a practical guide to using the information and techniques found within in order to create a better life and a better planet. Included in this book is an interactive instructional CD designed to be used in conjunction with the information in these pages. It will facilitate your ability to feel the power and energy of the Divine Name.

I have been personally engaged in sound healing since 1980, helping pioneer this field. In 1982, I founded the Sound Healers Association, the first organization dedicated to research on, and awareness of, the uses of sound and music for healing and transformation. Several years later, after studying and working with masters of sound from both the scientific and spiritual fields, I received a master's degree from Lesley University in Cambridge, Massachusetts, concentrating on this subject. Soon after, I began teaching this material for the first time. My study and research continue to this day, as do my personal discoveries. (I'm also the author of several classic, cutting-edge books on sound healing, including *Healing Sounds* and *The 7 Secrets of Sound Healing.* In addition, I've produced and created numerous best-selling and award-winning CDs, such as *Chakra Chants* and *2012: Ascension Harmonics.*)

In my investigation into this field, I've explored a wide variety of different modalities of sound that could positively shift and change the body, mind, and spirit—everything from modern scientific devices to ancient mystical instruments and chants, all reputed to create healing and transformation. Of all the vehicles for effecting positive change that I've encountered, the most potent has been the use of our own voice. And of all the ways of using our voice, the single most powerful sound that I've discovered and utilized has been that of the Divine Name. It is now my great honor to share this discovery with you.

The premise of *The Divine Name* is this: *there is a universal sound that when properly intoned can bring us harmony and healing on both a personal and a planetary level.* The fact that this vocalization is composed of vowels that can resonate both the physical body and subtle energy fields and that when properly intoned, it sounds strikingly like the personal name of God found in the Abrahamic traditions is purely coincidental. Or is it?

My purpose in writing this book is simple: to share what may be the most profound and advanced technique for healing and transformation that I've encountered. It's easy to use—no prior experience is necessary. It calls for no external mechanism and involves only your voice, heart, and spirit. It doesn't require extensive training—you'll be able to experience and utilize it in a matter of hours. And the users' manual—this book—is straightforward. Learning to sound the Divine Name will lead to a new consciousness, and a life-changing new way of being. This technology may even lead to a new level of evolution for the world.

Legend has it that proper and reverential sounding of the Divine Name could bring one into contact with the ultimate Divine Creator being itself. Some believe that the actual act of the universe's creation occurred with this sound. The Divine Name was once said to have been known, but this knowledge disappeared nearly 2,500 years ago. It became prohibited to sound the Divine Name when reading the Old Testament, the religious text that links more than half of the world's population. The Divine Name became secret, and then it became lost. No one knew how it was actually pronounced. Its sound became pure speculation.

What exactly *is* the Divine Name? In Hebrew, it is written as יהוה. This four-letter name of God is often referred to as the *Tetragrammaton.* It has been translated into English as *YHVH,* Yahweh, and even Jehovah. However, none of these are accurate. No one has known the correct name, since its exact pronunciation was lost millennia ago . . . that is, until now!

In truth, the Divine Name—the Tetragrammaton—as I interpret it, is composed purely of vowels. This sequence of vowels can resonate both the physical and subtle energy centers of anyone who intones it. Thus, the Divine Name is trans-denominational—applicable to all traditions of belief—and something that can be experienced by anyone who follows the simple guidelines of this book. You'll learn how *you* can utilize the Divine Name as an extraordinary tool for both personal and planetary healing and transformation.

The Divine Name requires no musical ability. Rather, it is a self-created sound that must be intoned in order to be experienced. It is the most extraordinary vibratory energy *I* have encountered in my more than 30 years of research and investigation into the field of sound healing. The ability to create this sound has *nothing* to do with musical ability. You don't need to read notes or understand music theory. You certainly don't need to be able to play an instrument. And you most definitely don't need to be a trained singer or even be able to carry a tune in a bucket in order to experience the power of the lost name of God.

The Divine Name is a step-by-step process of vibratory activation using sacred sound. It is divided into four parts:

— In **Part I**, you'll explore the discoveries and revelations of the Divine Name. You'll learn the complete story of how the sound of the Divine Name came to me, and what my explorations of the sacred texts of the Old Testament revealed about its validity, not only as vowel sounds but also as the personal name of God that was delivered to Moses. You'll understand how and why this most sacred of sounds became prohibited, then hidden, and finally lost. You'll realize why this secret and most venerated name needs to manifest now in the current world in which we live, and you'll find out what uncovering this forgotten sound can mean on both a personal and planetary level.

— In **Part II**, you'll explore the extraordinary power of sacred sound. You'll discover the scientific and spiritual aspects of sound for healing and self-transformation—focusing on the power of sound and consciousness and how various traditions on this planet regard sound as the original creative force. You'll delve into an exploration of the importance of intent and prayer to co-create reality. You'll also learn about the sacred vowels and their ability to resonate with, balance, and align our chakras from the Hindu tradition; and to channel Divine energies from the Kabbalistic traditions. You'll grow in awareness of how the Divine Name can be utilized for healing and self-transformation, and why the consciousness encoded upon this sound amplifies its power.

— **Part III** of *The Divine Name* is a step-by-step process of vibratory activation focusing on sonic exercises designed to teach you how to intone the Divine Name. You'll begin by experiencing the power of vowels to resonate your chakras, and progress to being able to sound the Divine Name using a special series of vowels. As previously noted, I've created an accompanying instructional CD that will allow you to hear the actual sounds you'll be working with, which will greatly enhance your learning process. This is an interactive recording, designed to be used in conjunction with Part III.

— **Part IV** of this book is its finale—the culmination of the purpose for learning to sound the Divine Name. Once you've mastered how to vocalize the Divine Name, you'll focus on the final step in receiving the ultimate benefit of the Divine Name: you will experience the power and majesty of this extraordinary sound as a tool for manifesting a new form of universal prayer for both personal and planetary healing and self-transformation.

In these pages, you'll encounter a journey of self-discovery that can change your life. With the revelation of the Divine Name and the technique of how to vocalize it, you'll be receiving one of the greatest gifts ever—the ability to understand and intone the personal name for God, which has been purposely hidden and prohibited and whose true sound disappeared for many thousands of years. It is a universal sound that all can experience—with extreme power for healing and transformation. It is now time to bring this name back and let it resonate through our hearts, minds, and spirit; and to help usher in a new era in human consciousness of love and peace.

I want to thank you for accompanying me on this journey into the realm of the Divine Name—first learning about the significance of this name, then about the power of sacred sound, and finally how to actually generate this sound yourself. I can assure you that it will be a most fascinating and life-changing experience. Together we will make this journey. Enjoy!

Part I

Discoveries
and
Revelations

Chapter One

In the Beginning

I remember as a child being with my parents in a synagogue on Yom Kippur, the highest of holy days of the Jewish year, looking at the prayer books and seeing the Hebrew word יהוה. Someone pointed at this word, composed of the Hebrew letters *Yod Hey Vav Hey* (written in English as *YHVH*), and in a hushed voice said: "That's the secret name of God. It's so special that whenever we come to it in prayer, we say 'Adonai' because this secret name can never be spoken."

The concept was breathtaking and awe inspiring! A chill went through my young body as I stared at the word. A secret name that could never be spoken? That was something I wouldn't forget. Years later, as my interest in this name continued, I was told by someone versed in Hebrew mysticism that the name יהוה was really pronounced "Yahweh."

Yahweh. Yahweh! Yahweh?

With bated breath I tried it: "Yahweh." My heart raced, but nothing very special happened. I tried it again: "Yahweh." My heart still raced, but I hadn't been struck by lightning . . . nor had I experienced enlightenment. I tried it a third time, and when still nothing happened, I shrugged and moved on with life, deciding this secret name wasn't what it was cracked up to be.

The Dream

Then, decades later, came the dream. The year was 1993. I had just spoken at the International Sound Colloquium in Epping, New Hampshire, presenting material on the uses of sound as a healing modality. Before returning to my home outside Boulder, Colorado, I visited with my dear friend and teacher Sarah Benson and her husband, Donald Beaman, in Chelmsford, Massachusetts, a suburb of Boston.

Sarah was the woman who had first initiated me into the power of sound more than a dozen years before, setting me on this path of sound healing. She continued to be my teacher, friend, and guide as I made my journey on this planet. I suppose it is only fitting that I should have had this experience of the Divine Name while at her home. My previous book, *The 7 Secrets of Sound Healing,* was dedicated to Sarah, whom I described as "The Divine Mother of Sound Healing." Nothing has changed since that dedication, except that Sarah has transited from this planet. I still feel her presence.

Years before this dream, I'd discovered a system of using specific vowel sounds to resonate the chakras. That had come to me on March 21, 1986. I remember the date well because I'd been engaged in a powerful meditation that had assisted in this discovery.

Please know that I wasn't alone or original in the idea of using the vowel sounds for chakra resonance—I'd drawn upon the knowledge and experience of others and simply modified some of these sounds in order to find a specific system that worked best for me.

In truth, I must admit that I don't remember the exact details of the dream I experienced at Sarah's. I just recall waking up and being "told" to write down the system of vowels that I'd developed back in the '80s to tone the seven chakras. This system—which I'd been teaching for many years to balance the chakras—utilized a particular sequence of vowel sounds in which I would begin sounding the first chakra, located at the base of the spine, going upward until the seventh chakra, at the top of the head, was reached.

The Sacred Sound

Awakening from the dream at Sarah's, I was told to sound the chakras in a specific order. I wrote down the new order of vowel sounds and examined what I'd written. It was simply a reversal of the normal routine I'd been teaching on an almost weekly basis, only with a bit of a twist: I would start at the crown chakra and go down to the root chakra, and then go back up to the crown chakra. In all my years of teaching this system, I'd never reversed the order by starting at the seventh chakra and going to the first. Nor had I taken a further step and gone back up to the seventh.

But what could be special about that? I had to try it. Two things immediately happened:

1. As I intoned the vowels in this new manner, I felt the energy go from the top of my head down to the bottom of my spine, and then back up to and out the top of my head.

2. I distinctly heard the name "Yahweh" in the elongated vowels I'd sounded.

In truth, I'd expected the first experience to occur, since I already knew about the vibratory relationship between vowels and the chakras. But I was absolutely astonished by the sonic revelation of the second experience. Somehow it seemed that

I'd stumbled upon, or been guided to, the correct vocalization of the Divine Name—the Tetragrammaton. In actuality, this wasn't a spoken word, but rather a sound composed of elongated vowels that had to be *intoned!*

I knew I'd discovered something big. Extremely important. Perhaps even earth-shattering. And it was so very, very sacred. If legends about it were correct, it might even be a sound that could change the world!

Just one question remained . . .

What Was I to Do?

My response was initially to do nothing. You might well be wondering why I would choose such a course. The answer is simple—I wanted to be responsible. I'd been taught that this was a name so powerful and sacred that it was never supposed to be spoken. As will be discussed in the next chapter, its pronunciation had been suppressed, banned, and ultimately lost for millennia. I needed to determine if the vocalization I'd discovered—the actual intonation of the Divine Name as vowel sounds, not as a spoken name—should be shared with others. It certainly was the most powerful sound I'd ever experienced, and represented what I perceived as being the embodiment of Divine Light and Love through Sound. I've always tried to be extremely responsible when teaching information and techniques about the power of sound. This was no exception.

I began to slowly share my discovery with several people, including my wife, Andi, and a few extremely attuned sound-healing students of mine. Their impression of the Divine Name was similar to what mine had initially been—that it was the most powerful sound for attuning with the Divine that they'd ever experienced. We all agreed that at the time it was too powerful to share.

I immediately committed to secrecy anyone with whom I shared this. While the sounding of the Divine Name was relatively easy and simple to teach, I declined to do so. It wasn't yet time. I didn't know exactly when that "time" would be, but I was sure I would know when it arrived.

The Gregg Braden Connection

Years passed without further revelation of the Divine Name to others. Then in 2004, I attended a weekend presentation by Gregg Braden. Gregg and I had met several years before through a mutual friend, James Twyman. I'd always appreciated the information and clarity of thought in Gregg's writings. In addition, after our initial meeting, we kept communicating and developed a deep resonance between us. We began a friendship that grew, and continues to grow, to this day.

Gregg had come to Denver to give a presentation based upon his latest book, *The God Code.* He invited Andi and me to be his guests at this program. The weekend began with a Friday-night multimedia lecture, and by the end, I was astounded by the material that had been covered. I turned to Andi and said, "I can't believe this—Gregg is teaching a form of Kabbalah to the public. This is remarkable!"

Kabbalah is Judeo-Christian mysticism. It is defined as a body of mystical teachings of rabbinical origin, often based on an esoteric interpretation of the Hebrew scriptures. The tradition of Kabbalah is claimed to have been handed down orally from Abraham, the patriarch not only of Judaism, but of Christianity and Islam as well. Thus, these three religions, whose followers account for more than half the world's population, are known as the *Abrahamic traditions.*

Kabbalah literally means "to receive," for that is how most of the mystics got their information—through receipt of Divine messages during meditation, in prayer, or while reading the Holy Scriptures. It's one of the most powerful spiritual approaches I've encountered. At the center of much of Kabbalah is the use of the Divine Name—the Tetragrammaton—as a vehicle to receive Divine inspiration during meditation and prayer.

The Divine Name and DNA

Gregg Braden's presentation focused on the Tetragrammaton and the discoveries he'd made about how this name could be changed and transduced through mathematics, chemistry, and other sciences to deliver a special message. This message, found within our DNA, was a brief sequence that translates in English as the words *God/Eternal within the body.* It was powerful information that stressed the universality of the Tetragrammaton. This universality was also part of my understanding of it. From my discovery, I knew that there was something quite powerful that could be added to illustrate this work. The missing piece was the sound.

If יהוה, as Gregg had discovered, was encoded in our DNA as the message "God/Eternal within the body," then experiencing the sound of this name would be an even greater dynamic power for anyone who heard it. I knew that sound affected our DNA, and I believed that listening to the Divine Name could further amplify and enhance the activation of יהוה in it.

When the workshop concluded on Sunday, Gregg, Andi, and I went out to dinner. It was there that I suggested an idea to Gregg. I began by telling him about my discovery many years before that the Divine Name was in reality a sequence of vowel sounds. I told him that while I needed to meditate on it, I might be willing to make a recording of this sound for him to use during his presentations so that the audience could actually experience and feel the power of the Divine Name. Gregg agreed.

My First Recording

Gathering all my creative and intuitive abilities, I began recording the sound of the Divine Name. I had no idea how it would be received. In this most sacred of recordings, I was extremely reverent as I sounded the personal name of the Divine, so that all who heard it would experience its magnificence.

The end result was quite profound. I felt that somehow I'd done justice to my desire to create something that would honor the power of the Divine Name. The sound was both sacred and beautiful. I was satisfied that I'd manifested an adequate creation of the Tetragrammaton as I believed it should be sounded.

I played the recording for Gregg, who was quite moved by it. He thought that, indeed, by listening to the recording, his audience would be aided in experiencing the Divine, and it would add to their understanding of it. We agreed, however, that he would share this recording only during his presentations, and it wasn't to be reproduced. Gregg told me that when he played it in his workshops, he would request that all recording equipment be turned off by all participants.

When Gregg and I next spoke after one of his workshops, he excitedly related that there had been an overwhelmingly positive response from his audience upon hearing the recording. It seemed to spark something powerful and sacred in people. Some reported spiritual experiences. Others described healings. The responses all seemed most encouraging. I was delighted.

Then came the requests by participants for copies of the actual recording, but as we had agreed, the Divine Name wasn't to be reproduced. While it was being played, all recording equipment was turned off. Or so we thought.

Someone at one of Gregg's presentations hadn't honored the request to turn off such devices. It could have been a pocket recorder that simply kept recording when the Divine Name played. It didn't matter. The end result was that a poor-fidelity version began appearing on the Internet; a low-quality mono recording had manifested. There was only one thing to do— rather than have this inferior representation of the Divine Name circulate on the Web, it was imperative to release a high-quality version as a CD.

The Divine Name: Sounds of the God Code

I went into my recording studio to begin experimentation, and created the CD *The Divine Name: Sounds of the God Code.*

Several weeks later, in addition to the initial five-minute recording I'd made for Gregg's workshops, I created an hour-long musical composition that encompassed the Divine Name within a flowing bed of chanting voices. The result was quite enthralling.

Gregg and I worked together on the comprehensive liner notes of the CD, and it was then released through Hay House. The reception to this recording was excellent, and reports from listeners about the extraordinary effects of *The Divine Name* continue to this day.

The release of, and response to, the CD gave me the impetus to go where I hadn't gone before—contemplating actually *teaching* how to sound the Divine Name in a workshop. Could I safely, respectfully, and effectively share the information and techniques of this process publicly to an audience? It was something I'd put off for more than a decade. Was it now time to act?

I'd found Gregg's teachings on the Tetragrammaton and the material in *The God Code* to be extraordinary, and I decided that an audience who had received these teachings from him would be the perfect group with whom to share my information. I offered this as a suggestion to Gregg, and he felt it appropriate to have me present a workshop on the day following the conclusion of his presentation.

Teaching the Divine Name

Thus began a small series of workshops called "Sounding the Divine Name," which I taught on the Sunday after Gregg's Friday-evening and Saturday presentation. Much of the material is the basis for this book. Many people at these workshops have told me that my teachings were life changing—safe yet profound. I was quite happy and content with this—that is, until my inner guidance pushed my very resistant self toward taking the discovery a step further by writing a book that would not only impart an understanding of, but also the ability to sound, the Divine Name.

Those who may know of my past interests, activities, and accomplishments in the arena of sound healing are aware that for many years I've been dedicated to reawakening the power of sound and music for healing and transformation. I've focused on this power for personal healing, and within the last decade I've expanded this focus to include *planetary* healing and transformation. Teaching the Divine Name seemed to be a natural progression of my work. What better way to assist in the healing and evolution of this planet than to utilize the most sacred and powerful sound I'd ever encountered?

It is my belief that through sound, coupled with conscious intent, we can heal not only ourselves but the planet as well. Thus, I've been heavily involved with global sound-healing events, including World Sound Healing Day, in which people all over the world "sound" together, projecting the energy of peace and compassion over the earth. I termed this process of creating peace and harmony on the planet *Global Harmonization.* I also developed the Temple of Sacred Sound, the world's first interactive Website where people can go to tone for planetary peace and healing 24/7. (I'll offer more information about this later.)

For several years, I continued contemplating a revelation of the uses of the Divine Name for personal and planetary healing, especially because as time has gone by, it has become more and more apparent to me that there are some very powerful changes occurring on this planet. As an example, people started to become aware of a date—2012—which had been found in many different prophecies and traditions, including the Mayan calendar. This was said to be a crucial time of great global shift and change.

If listening to the sound of the Divine Name helped encode the awareness of "God/Eternal within the body," learning to vocalize this name with our own voice could potentially activate and align our DNA to higher levels of evolutionary development. Perhaps for those who were truly able to resonate with the energy of the Divine Name, such sounding could even offer greater abilities and consciousness, enhancing personal and planetary peace and harmony.

This was a sound that could help generate compassion and oneness. It could initiate attunement with the Divine. Perhaps we needed to have the power of the Divine Name at this time in order for these higher qualities of consciousness to manifest. To me, it seemed so natural and very important to unveil it. My only problem was the trepidation I felt. I was hesitant, thinking that this was a name not to be publicly revealed but to be kept secret and hidden—that it was too sacred. While I'd slowly begun to work with others, I hadn't yet done research into the ancient scriptures—an investigation that revealed the Divine Name as one to be remembered, but not misused.

Meditation on Yom Kippur

Then something extraordinary happened.

It was Yom Kippur of 2008. Yom Kippur is the single most important holiday in the Hebrew tradition. Translated as "Day of Atonement," it is the time when Jewish people ask forgiveness for any mistakes committed throughout the year. During prayer, they seek to awaken the Divine within themselves in order to find release and make amends, fixing whatever errors have been committed. It is not only a time of atonement, but of "attunement"— of being at one with the Divine.

On Yom Kippur, it is said that the veils between the planes of existence open up. In legend, it was the one day of the year when the high priests in the Temple of Jerusalem were allowed to sound the Tetragrammaton—the Divine Name.

On this particular Yom Kippur, I was in deep contemplation of the Divine Name and its potential revelation in a book such as this. Was such a revelation proper and correct? Was it in alignment with the Divine? I was praying and meditating outdoors when I distinctly heard a voice that spoke these words: *It is time to revive My Name, lest it be forgotten.*

Immediately after I heard this, I began my research into the sacred scriptures. I found that the message I received seems to echo the experience of Moses and his encounter with the burning bush, which revealed that the Tetragrammaton was ". . . the name by which I am to be remembered from generation to generation." For me, this experience during meditation on Yom Kippur was a Divine revelation, and one whose dictate I'm fulfilling now by penning these pages. The powerful and clear message that I received was an affirmation, as well as a direct statement and declaration, to write *The Divine Name.* Because of this message, I like to think that this book is a divinely inspired project.

Tikkun Olam

During the research and writing of this book, I came across the concept of *Tikkun Olam,* Hebrew words that translate as "repairing or mending of the world." Tikkun Olam refers to an acknowledgment that things are out of balance on the earth, and the importance of restoring peace and harmony to the planet. Tikkun Olam is part of an ancient myth of creation in which Divine Light became shattered and scattered. While most of the Light returned to its Divine Source, some did not. It is therefore the duty of spiritual beings to return all these sparks to Source. In doing so, we can repair the world.

For many, Tikkun Olam is the basic principle of the Kabbalah—the purpose behind mystical studies of the Bible. For what other reason should someone seek enlightenment if not to make the world a better place through fixing what may be broken? On a personal level, Tikkun Olam often involves acts of compassion and kindness. However, on a more expansive and universal level, it literally means *Global Harmonization*—my vision of incorporating sound to create peace and harmony on the planet.

It became apparent to me that this was yet another confirmation that the Divine Name was not only meant to be rediscovered, but ultimately to be used as a universal sound to assist the earth at this time.

❖✖❖

Thank you for allowing me to recount my personal story of my journey with the Divine Name and ultimately how this book came to be written. In the following chapters, we'll begin to delve more deeply into the history of the Divine Name. This will give us a better understanding of the depth and breadth inherent in it, and better facilitate our ability to resonate with this name together.

Chapter Two

By This Name Shall I Be Known

The most popular book in the world is the Bible. It is composed of two different volumes, commonly referred to as the Old Testament and New Testament. These are in turn actually a compilation of numerous books from the Hebrew and Christian traditions.

Readers find extraordinary solace and comfort in the pages of the Bible. Many believe that despite different translations in numerous languages, the Bible is the "Word of God." Yet few know that there is a sacred name—in fact, the *most* sacred and powerful one of all: the personal name of God, which was never spoken or sounded.

What Is יהוה?

So, what is this name? It is the personal name of God first revealed to Moses during his encounter with the burning bush on Mount Sinai. In Hebrew it is written as יהוה (this language is read from right to left—not left to right, as in English), composed of the Hebrew letters *Yod Hey Vav Hey.* In English, this has been translated as *YHVH.* It is often pronounced *Yahweh.*

יהוה is the word for this personal name of God. As I explained in the Introduction, these Hebrew letters are universally known in spiritual traditions as the *Tetragrammaton,* a Greek word meaning the four-letter name of God. Throughout this book, "Divine Name" and "Tetragrammaton" will be used interchangeably.

After the revelation of this personal name of God to Moses, it is said that the people of Israel knew about this appellation, the Divine Name, and utilized it in their sacred prayers. Then about 400 to 600 years before the birth of Christ, for reasons unknown, the use of this name was prohibited. It became blasphemy for it to be spoken by any except the high priests in Israel on a specific holy day of the year. The penalty for transgressions was severe!

A Jew who encountered the letters יהוה (YHVH) in reading the scriptures aloud was directed to say "Adonai" (Lord), "Ha-Shem" (the Name), or another substitute in place of the Divine Name. The real personal name indicated by the letters יהוה was never vocalized. Soon after this ban, the true sound of the Divine Name became lost.

The True Revelation

It is commonly believed that the personal name revealed to Moses during his first encounter with the burning bush was "Ehyeh asher ehyeh." This Hebrew statement is most frequently translated as "I am that I am," "I am he who is," or "I will be what is needed of me" (there are numerous other versions). It certainly is the opening reference that Moses is given when he asks to whom he is speaking.

However, further reading of the words spoken by God to Moses at this time reveals that "Ehyeh asher ehyeh" is not the true Divine Name but something else—a depiction of the quality of God, but not His name. God is telling Moses, "I am everything." It is far from a personal name.

In Exodus 3:13, when facing the burning bush, Moses asks who he should tell his people he has spoken with. The first reply is indeed "Ehyeh asher ehyeh." However, a complete reading of the incident reveals startlingly important information. Another statement declares that יהוה—YHVH—is the personal name of God. This revelation of the Divine Name is found immediately following the reference to "Ehyeh asher ehyeh." Here is the complete revelation as described in the New Jerusalem Bible, which uses "Yahweh" when יהוה is written in the Hebrew Torah:

> Moses then said to God, "If I go to the Israelites and say to them, 'The God of your ancestors has sent me to you,' and they say to me, 'What is his name?' what am I to tell them?"
> God said to Moses, "I am he who is." And he said, "This is what you are to say to the Israelites, 'I am has sent me to you.'"
> God further said to Moses, "You are to tell the Israelites, 'Yahweh, the God of your ancestors, the God of Abraham, the God of Isaac and the God of Jacob, has sent me to you.' This is my name for all time, and thus I am to be invoked for all generations to come."

In this important passage, we understand that not only does God give his personal name to Moses, but instructs him that this name is to be carried forward for all subsequent generations. *It is a name to be remembered!* We can actually interpret *not* using the Divine Name as failing to obey God's instructions. This original biblical text suggests that to use any name other than God's personal one in our prayers of healing, peace, and life is a dishonoring of the Divine Name itself.

Thus YHVH (יהוה) is the true name revealed to Moses—this is the one to be both invoked and remembered. It is neither an attribute, such as God Almighty or God the Merciful, nor a description, such as "I am everything" or "I am all that is." It is the personal name by which to call the Creator, and its power was said to be extraordinary.

With an awareness of the personal name of God, it's possible to properly utilize this sound in order to experience and resonate with the energy of the Divine. There are many mythic stories about the powers and abilities inherent in this name—some even say it was the original sound of creation.

The Name Becomes Lost

According to legend and tradition, the Divine Name was known to the original people of Israel and was used by them. This is the same name that was suppressed and the vocalization of which was ultimately prohibited. After centuries of being conquered and dispersed by other tribes and traditions, the Israelites lost the true pronunciation of the Divine Name. The real sound of יהוה disappeared. How could this have happened?

Modern Hebrew is a language without any specific vowel sounds. It is commonly believed that all the words in the original Torah (Hebrew for the first five books of the Old Testament) were simply consonants with no vowels. Thus, when reading the Torah, people could encounter problems in pronunciation.

Imagine if I wrote the consonants *ct*—this could be read and pronounced as either "cat," "cut," or "cot." As you can see, using three different vowels creates three very different-sounding words from these consonants. Each of these three words also has a very different meaning.

The Torah was most frequently transmitted through an oral tradition. A Jew was supposed to know it so well that when he came upon a word, he would recognize what it was because he had been taught it through constant exposure to the sounds— usually through the repetition of sacred text.

But if a word was suppressed or forbidden, how would you know its true sound? What if you weren't allowed to vocalize a word? How could you know what it was? After centuries of not being allowed to pronounce the Name, it seems obvious that one would lose direct understanding of how that name was to be sounded. No one knows exactly when, but the actual vocalization of the Divine Name became lost.

Many sources suggest that "Yahweh" may have been the pronunciation, but this is just a guess. There are many other guesses, such as "Jehovah," which is actually a translation of יהוה first into Greek and then into Latin. In contemporary Hebrew, vowel sounds are created by a series of dots and dashes known as *vowel points,* which were added to the text in order to standardize the pronunciation of the words. This happened around A.D. 700. Before that standardization, pronunciation of the Torah occurred through oral information being passed down from generation to generation.

So due to the prohibition of the Divine Name and its lack of use, its pronunciation became lost. But why had its sounding been prohibited at all? One of the great mysteries with regard to the Divine Name was *why* it became banned.

Why the Name Became Banned

In the liner notes of *The Divine Name: Sounds of the God Code,* Gregg Braden tells us:

> Fear of uttering the Divine Name was so great at times that oaths were taken in order to avoid God's wrath. It should be emphasized here that these concerns and fears are human interpretations of the ancient texts, rather than instructions that accompany the Divine Name in the texts themselves.

Mundane circumstances rather than spiritual edicts may be at the root of this mystery. Quite often, information is made secret or is restricted as a means of control. It is usually prohibited as a means for one group of people to hold power over another group of people. One school of thought holds that in the case of the Tetragrammaton, its use was prohibited by order of the priest class in Jerusalem.

Donald Tyson speculates in *The Power of the Word:*

> The reason for the restriction of the Name is not known. . . . I tend to believe it was connected with a growing social gulf between the priest class and the people. The priests reserved the name exclusively as the supreme emblem of their authority, in very much the same way that the Catholic Church of the Middle Ages bitterly resisted the translation of the Bible into the common tongues of Europe. Knowledge is power.

Perhaps the suppression of the Tetragrammaton had been enforced to keep the people from the wonderment of experiencing personal connection with God. Donald Beaman, the author of *The Tarot of Saqqara,* echoes these thoughts:

> The Divine Name was so powerful, it enabled those who knew it to have direct connection with the Source of all that is. With this proper use of this sound, the people could have their own access to God. The priesthood became unnecessary. This threatened them and as a result the Tetragrammaton became banned.

Being able to separate the people from the extraordinary energy of the Divine Name may indeed have been a reason why it became prohibited. The 2nd-century Torah scholar Rabbi Pinchas ben Yair says: "Why do people pray without being answered? Because they do not know how to use the explicit Name."

After my own revelation of the Divine Name on Yom Kippur, I began to vigorously investigate why the suppression of the Tetragrammaton may have occurred and been enforced. As speculated previously, one reason might have been to keep the people from the majesty of being able to experience a personal connection with God by sounding His name.

From the Torah

Yet, as Gregg Braden notes, in several parts of the Torah, we are told that God's personal name is the only name of God that we are to offer in our prayers. In Deuteronomy 10:20, it reads: ". . . by his [Yahweh your God's] name shall you swear."

This same implication—that to use anything other than the Divine Name in our prayers of healing is a dishonoring of God—is found in Deuteronomy 6:13, where it states: ". . . him shall you serve, and shall swear by his name."

Gregg writes:

> The English translation of such phrases invites a clarification of precisely what it means to "swear" by a particular name. From *The American Heritage Dictionary* we are shown that to swear is "to make a solemn declaration, invoking a deity or some person or thing held sacred, in confirmation of the honesty or truth of such a declaration." Thus, the passages of the Torah instruct us that it is only in the personal name of God, in the honesty and truth of the name YHVH, that we make our solemn declarations of prayer.

From the Ten Commandments

Perhaps the strongest and most important dictate regarding the instructions on the use of the Divine Name occurs in the Torah, in the simplicity and clarity of the Ten Commandments given to Moses by the Supreme Being in Exodus 20:7. An examination of this passage suggests the importance of using this name, and yet another possible reason for the prohibition of the Divine Name also manifests. What if the prohibition against using it was an attempt to somehow protect it? In the New Jerusalem Bible translation, we are told: "You shall not misuse the name of Yahweh your God . . ."

Here the Creator deems His name so important that it is presented as one of ten major commandments that have guided Western consciousness and morality since they were first received. *We are not told to stop using it.* There is no prohibition against the Divine Name. However, the end of this commandment does warn that any misuse of it will lead to retribution by Yahweh. Thus, we aren't forbidden to use it, but we are strongly guided to avoid *mis*use of it.

What *is* considered misuse of the Divine Name? In various translations of this commandment, other phrasings of *misuse* include: "profanity or cursing"; "futilely," "without proper reverence or intent," "inappropriately," "without honor," and "for an evil purpose"; "idly utter," "use lightly," and "make false promises"; and "irreverently" and "in vain."

Thus, the scope of what constitutes misuse of the Divine Name is enormous in magnitude. What is correct use, and what is incorrect use, of this extraordinary name?

In his book *Magic of the Ordinary*, Rabbi Gershon Winkler, a renowned Jewish scholar, focuses on the practical use of spiritual energies in Judaism. He tells us that improper use is "the misuse of supernal powers to take advantage of people and to intimidate them," while proper use "involves the channeling of supernal powers to heal, to uplift, and to do so with the awareness that the Creator is the ultimate source of all these feats." He further informs us that as long as it is in alignment with the Divine, "a supernatural occurrence invoked by chanting the Sacred Name constitutes no disruption of the order of the physical universe" and is therefore acceptable and appropriate use of this name.

From a very personal perspective, this feels extremely accurate. The most sacred sound imaginable, as taught in this book, can manifest only positive applications. Ultimately, through correct use, we are guided to honor this extraordinary name in all our dealings with it.

Not a Word, but a <u>Sound</u>

As I'll explain in later chapters, in order to properly sound the Divine Name, it cannot simply be spoken; rather, it must be *intoned*. It is not a word, but a sound—a Divine sound composed of a series of elongated vowels. Ordinary speech doesn't come close to embodying the power inherent in the true vocalization of the Divine Name. Saying "Yahweh," or any of the other numerous versions of the Tetragrammaton, is merely a pale imitation of the majesty of sounding the Divine Name.

In order to use this sound to its full potency, we need to employ a number of different modalities in this vocalization, including our thoughts, feelings, and breath. In the true understanding and sounding of the Divine Name found in this book, it becomes ineffectual, if not impossible, to use it in any manner other than for the highest good of all. It's almost as though there is a "fail-safe" mechanism built into the sounding of the Tetragrammaton that doesn't allow misuse to occur. Once we understand and know the feeling of creating the Divine Name and then experience it, it can only be utilized in alignment with all that is holy!

In the Torah, the Holy Scriptures, we're presented with two major directives about the Divine Name: we are told (1) that it is a name that is to be remembered, and (2) that it is not to be misused. Thus, this book is a vehicle to restore the awareness and memory of the Divine Name, as well as to present the proper use of it as a sacred and holy sound.

Chapter Three

The Divine Name as Vowels

My discovery that the Divine Name—the Tetragrammaton—was composed entirely of vowels came to me through a dream, but the guidance I received would have meant nothing without my years of experience working with and teaching the transformational and healing power of sound. This revelation of the Divine Name wasn't due to any specific reading, or being told something in hushed whispers at a meeting of some secret society.

As you may recall, as I awakened from this dream, I was given instructions to intone the precise vowel sounds that I'd been utilizing for many years in the specific sound-healing exercises that

I taught. I was guided to intone them in a particular order—in a manner I'd never done before. It was that simple and that different and that life changing.

Honoring Other Sounds

When I sounded the vowels in the given sequence, I heard the Divine Name. At that time, I knew with total certainty that this was a correct way of vocalizing יהוה. Please note, though, that while I do believe that the information I'm presenting is correct—that the Divine Name is the lost sound of God—I don't necessarily feel it is the *only* way of sounding the Tetragrammaton. There are any number of other techniques to do this that work for some people. My own experience has taught me to honor the resonances that others have experienced using sound—particularly sacred sound. If there's one thing I've learned, it's that there is no "absolute" or "one and only" sound, tone, or frequency that will always resonate the same way for everyone.

Nevertheless, I will acknowledge that in the many years I've spent exploring sacred sound from throughout the world, the Divine Name is the most powerful example I've ever encountered. It is the embodiment of what I consider to be Divine Light and Love as Sound. Thus, I share my experience of the universality of the Divine Name with you so that you may feel its extraordinary resonance as well.

The Sound of the Vowels

Interestingly, the sound I distinctly heard when intoning the vowels in the order I received after my dream was clearly "Yahweh." As previously noted, I was quite shocked and awed and impressed. It wasn't as though the guidance that had directed me to vocalize the vowels in that particular sequence had said, "Sound the vowels in this manner and you will hear the Tetragrammaton." It didn't. It simply suggested that I tone the vowels in a specific order.

As discussed in the previous chapter, Kabbalah is the mystical aspect of the Abrahamic traditions—Judaism, Christianity, and Islam—and its literal meaning is "to receive." From my perspective, what occurred when I was guided to sound the vowels in order to generate the Divine Name was certainly an aspect of receiving. This is the way much information comes to me—in a "lightning bolt" flash. Then I often have to spend much time—sometimes years—researching the information and attempting to validate and prove its authenticity. Such was the case with my initial experience of the Divine Name.

It might have been easier for me if I'd encountered the sound while simultaneously being given references to different books that would corroborate my experience. However, this wasn't the case. Exploring different avenues that would ultimately lead me to verification of the Divine Name as being composed exclusively of vowels was obviously part of my process.

Permutations of the Tetragrammaton

Most Kabbalistic practice focuses on presenting the student with opportunities for advancing spiritually, attuning with God, and ultimately achieving enlightenment. One of the most common exercises is to use the Tetragrammaton, יהוה, as a tool for deep inner resonance and for merging with the Divine. Since actual pronunciation of the Divine Name was considered impossible, an alternative method has been to sound the names of the Hebrew letters in different permutations. Chanting various combinations of the Yod, the Hey, and the Vav is considered one of the most potent Kabbalistic practices for achieving enlightenment. Pioneered by the Kabbalistic rabbi Abraham Abulafia, the technique of chanting these permutations is said to be among the most powerful and effective ever developed.

Something More . . .

In my Kabbalistic studies in the past, I'd taken part in this practice of chanting the permutations of the Tetragrammaton letters: the Yod, the Hey, and the Vav. I will acknowledge that it is an extraordinary practice—deeply meditative and consciousness-shifting. But it was, for me at least, not very different from the experience of chanting mantras from other traditions that incorporated repetition of syllables or words. I still believed that there was more to the Tetragrammaton than simply working with sounding these consonants. I did not, however, know what that something more was.

Then I awakened from the dream and received instructions to sound specific vowels in a specific order. When I did so, and heard the name Yahweh—the Divine Name, the Tetragrammaton—my world was forever changed.

Indeed, while I'd experimented with the practice of chanting the Hebrew consonants of the Tetragrammaton and found it powerful, this paled in comparison to my experience of vocalizing the vowel sounds in the aftermath of my dream. This was nothing less than the *most* powerful sound I had ever encountered, allowing me to feel the energy enter the top of my head, go to the base of my spine, and then return through the top of my head. It was nothing less than a transcendent experience.

What about the Vowels?

My one difficulty with this approach to sounding the Tetragrammaton, however, was simply that the sounds I'd created while intoning the Divine Name had been composed solely of vowels. There were no consonants present. As far as I knew at the time, the Hebrew alphabet was made up entirely of consonants—there were no vowel letters. What had I heard? It was most disconcerting and confusing.

On one level, I was puzzled by the similarity between the vocalization I'd created using only vowels and the sound "Yahweh." On another level, though, I was confronted with the fact that while my sounding might have seemed similar to the Tetragrammaton, they couldn't have been the same, since to my knowledge, there were no vowel letters in the Hebrew alphabet.

At the time, I didn't know that indeed there were systems of study validating my experience that the Divine Name was composed completely of vowels. It would take quite a while for me to find this out. Thus, I continued happily on my path through my Kabbalistic studies for several years, dismissing all I'd experienced with the Divine Name as having been unrelated to the Tetragrammaton . . . that is, until I tried to learn Hebrew.

The Vowels Begin to Appear

I knew that it was my duty as a student of Jewish mysticism to learn Hebrew—a language I'd always found difficult. One day, I picked up a little book called *Teach Yourself Biblical Hebrew* by R. K. Harrison.

I'd gotten through the first few chapters of the book with no difficulty. Then, as I came to the information presented in the chapter on the *vowels* of the Hebrew language, I did a double take. I held my breath in awe as I read on. This book stated that until the 6th century B.C., there were actually three letters in the Hebrew alphabet that had also served as vowels.

I was astounded by this. The writer of the book wasn't from some strange mystical cult, but rather from a seminary affiliated with the University of Toronto. There had to be something to this. I continued to investigate the theory that certain of the Hebrew letters had once actually been vowels. After I'd made this discovery, it didn't take much further exploration for me to find out that while this knowledge wasn't well known, it was there for anyone to uncover.

The text of the Bible was originally written with only the 22 letters of the Hebrew alphabet. About 1,000 years ago, a series of "vowel points" were added to the Hebrew language in order to standardize pronunciation and understanding of the Torah. This was done by a group of priestly scribes called the Masoretes, who created a system of dots and dashes known as *nikkud,* which were placed below the Hebrew consonants to represent the vowels. But what about before that time?

Examination of the Dead Sea Scrolls, which date back at least 2,000 years, indicates that there were several Hebrew letters used as vowels. Then something happened. At some point between the writing of the Dead Sea Scrolls and the nikkud of the Masoretes, the vowel letters of the Hebrew alphabet ceased to be. No one knows why. When the Masoretes reinserted the vowel points into the text, this did create an exact pronunciation of the Hebrew, but it was a rather modern addition. It wasn't ancient Hebrew.

The Vowels in the Tetragrammaton

Through a strange twist of fate, I'd discovered that there were several letters in the Hebrew alphabet that had initially acted as vowels. So what were these mysterious consonants that were once also vowel sounds? They were the same letters of the alphabet as those found in the Tetragrammaton—יהוה—the Yod, the Hey, and the Vav.

This realization was quite startling to me. The Tetragrammaton—the Divine Name—in its ancient Hebrew form had originally been sounded as vowels! Continued research revealed that it wasn't simply the *Teach Yourself Biblical Hebrew* book that talked about this, but also many other scholarly sources I consulted, from *The Ancient Hebrew Lexicon of the Bible* by Jeff A. Benner to *Hebrew Tutor,* a modern-day interactive CD-ROM with text by Ted Hildebrandt.

Even more extraordinary was the discovery that certain sources suggested that the letter ה (the Hey) was pronounced slightly differently in its two different positions—as an "AH" sound at the beginning of the name, and as an "AYE" (as in "may," not "my") at the end of the name. These sources included Josephus, the 1st-century Hebrew historian; Fabre d'Olivet, a 19th-century scholar cited in Joscelyn Godwin's *The Mystery of the Seven Vowels;* and Charles William Wall's linguistic text *Proofs of the Interpolation of the Vowel-Letters in the Text of the Hebrew Bible.*

Thus, the vowels resulting from intoning יהוה by pronouncing ה as two different sounds were: EEE—AH—OOO—AYE. When I tried this myself for the first time, I heard the same sound I'd vocalized the morning when I awakened from my dream. I clearly heard the Divine Name. My inner guidance and experience had now been validated and authenticated for me.

Professor Leonora Leet of St. John's University writes in *The Secret Doctrine of Kabbalah:*

> It is surprising that no grammarian who has discussed the vowel-letters has noted the signal fact, which should be apparent to any intelligent five year old (especially if he has already begun to study Hebrew), that the vowel-letters are the very letters of the Tetragrammaton!

While the modern Hebrew alphabet is composed only of consonants, it appears that ancient Hebrew indeed had vowels. While knowledge of this is more arcane—reserved for scholars and the like—it nevertheless is true and valid.

When and why the pronunciation of יהוה (the Yod, Hey, and Vav) was altered from being vowel letters remains a mystery. For whatever reason, this did in fact occur, and the original sounding of the Tetragrammaton as vowel sounds became unknown. The true sound of the Divine Name vanished.

Feeling the Divine Name

As previously shared, I was guided to create a recording of the Divine Name as vowels. Upon experiencing this recording, Gregg Braden understood yet another aspect of the power of the Tetragrammaton. In the liner notes of *The Divine Name: Sounds of the God Code,* he explains:

> On a *feeling level* . . . the experience of *hearing* the Divine Name carries a special and unique significance for a number of reasons. Because it's intoned as the vowels that unite rather than the consonants that divide (a phenomenon that linguists describe as the Tower of Babel between alphabets), the Divine Name is a truly universal and sacred tone. The power of this name is that it transcends languages, borders, bloodlines, beliefs, and lifestyles.

The vowels and their corresponding letters are pure sonics, with no consonants to initiate differences between peoples, races, traditions, countries, and so on. Jonathan illustrates this phenomenon by describing the Divine Name as "the sequence of vowel sounds manifesting the harmonics series in a descending and ascending pattern that energetically affects our body, mind, and spirit. This name transcends language, and without language, the barriers of separations cease to exist. I believe the Divine Name may be a rediscovery of an ancient universal vibration that will benefit all of humankind."

Regardless of how we live our lives or what we believe, the sight and sound of the God Code reminds us that we are a family.

It is this precise understanding of the universality of the vowel sounds, and thus the universality of the Divine Name, that may be among the most important ideas for us to be aware of. The Tetragrammaton may initially seem to stem from the Abrahamic religions, but in truth this name, composed of vowel sounds, is trans-denominational—found within any and all traditions.

When I first vocalized the Divine Name, I felt the sound come from the top of my head, go through my body and energy centers to the base of my spine, and then go back through the top of my head. It was an indescribable experience. This phenomenon continues to this day when I vocalize this extraordinary sound. As the personal name of God, this is a sound that is so powerful that it brings spirit into matter, and then transforms back into spirit.

The Divine Name is a universal sound that with proper teaching may be experienced by everyone in a similar fashion. Its universality has the potential to create a sense of oneness that can help unify this planet and its people.

The next section deals with the power of sound and mantras, and in particular, of vowel sounds and their corresponding harmonics. I'll share how these vowel sounds relate to both the physical body and its corresponding subtle energy centers, and begin to explore the reality of my experience as I sounded the Divine Name.

Let us journey now into the realm of sacred sound and see what awaits us.

Part II

Sacred Sound

Chapter Four

Exploring Sacred Sound

$\mathcal{F}$or those of you who know my work, some of the information and exercises that follow may seem familiar. But this material takes on a totally new life with the Divine Name as our focal point for learning about the extraordinary healing and transformational power of sound. Whether you're an adept at sound or a total neophyte in this field, the material covered will be of great benefit. The sonic insights you'll receive in this step-by-step initiation will ultimately lead you to a place where you can gain the ability to intone the Divine Name.

This is my sixth published book related to the healing and transformational uses of sound. Each one has contained information from the various spiritual and religious traditions on this planet, and the belief that the original act of creation occurred through sound. However, never before has the statement "In the beginning was the Word" had quite so much meaning for me.

Sound in the Beginning

If you examine the basic tenets of the world's various spiritual traditions, you find a common thread in their understanding that the universe was brought into being through sound. Indeed, according to John in the New Testament, God, creation, and sound are one: "In the beginning was the Word: the Word was with God and the Word was God."

From Genesis in the Old Testament we read: "And God said, 'Let there be light.'" Here, we are told of the manifestation of light occurring through the Creator speaking—making sound.

From the Upanishads of the Hindu tradition comes the writing: "By God's utterance came the universe."

The ancient Egyptians believed that the god Thoth created the world by his voice alone.

The Hopi creation story tells us that Spider Woman sang the song of creation over the inanimate forms on this planet and gave them life.

All of the major religions on this planet, as well as the esoteric, spiritual, and indigenous traditions, share a commonality of understanding that the fundamental creative force was vibration—the energy of sound.

In addition to the sacred texts describing sound as the major force of manifestation, the ancient mystery schools that existed thousands of years ago in Rome, Athens, Egypt, India, China, and Tibet had vast knowledge of the power of sound to heal. The various writings that have survived from those times indicate that in these schools, the use of sound as a therapeutic tool was a highly developed spiritual science, based on an understanding that vibration was the fundamental creative force of the universe.

In India, Vedic texts thousands of years old tell us, "Nada Brahman"—the world is sound! The words of these ancients are now being echoed by our greatest scientists, such as quantum physicist Michio Kaku, who has declared: "Everything is music." Modern physicists, in fact, postulate *string theory*—the idea that this and other dimensions are actually composed of tiny strings that vibrate at different rates.

Everything Is Sound

Science and spirituality are in agreement. In the beginning, depending upon what system you examine, it may be called the "Word," "big bang," or "cosmic hum." Regardless of the name, it amounts to the same thing—sound as the original creative force. Our ancient mystics and our modern physicists tell us the same thing: everything is sound.

What is sound? It is vibration. On a fundamental level of physics, this vibrational energy travels as waves, which are measured in cycles per second—scientifically referred to as hertz (Hz). The number of waves that occur per second is known as a sound's *frequency*. We hear from about 20 Hz to about 20,000 Hz. However, it's important to know that sound occurs over a much wider range than that which we can hear—dolphins, for example, can send and receive information at upwards of 180,000 Hz. These sonic vibrations are nearly ten times greater than our own highest level of hearing. It's essential that we conceive of sound not merely as those frequencies that fall within our audible bandwidth, but as something much greater. Just because we may be unable to hear something doesn't mean a sound isn't being created.

Everything is in a state of vibration, and therefore everything is sound—from electrons moving around the nucleus of an atom to planets in distant galaxies revolving around stars. The pages of this book are vibrating. So is the chair you may be sitting in. So is your body.

Principles of Sound Healing

The specific rate at which an object vibrates is known as its *resonant frequency*. All the various parts of the body—our organs, bones, tissues, and different systems—have their own specific frequencies. When we're in a state of health, we're like an extraordinary orchestra playing beautiful music together, creating this wonderful "Suite of the Self." All parts of us are balanced and in harmony. In fact, we often call this condition of balance and harmony *sound* health.

But what happens if the second-violin player in this orchestra loses his sheet music? He begins to play the wrong notes. He isn't only playing out of tune, but also out of time, resulting in the wrong harmony, melody, and rhythm. It sounds awful! Soon the entire string section is off. Before long, this one string player affects the entire orchestra.

This situation with the string player who has lost his sheet music is analogous to a portion of the body that has lost its natural, healthy resonance and is vibrating out of harmony and out of ease. We call this condition "dis-ease." Traditional allopathic medicine currently deals with this metaphorical string player who has lost his sheet music with one of two approaches: (1) giving this poor individual enough drugs that he passes out; or else (2), analogous to surgery, cutting off his head with a sword.

With either approach, you've temporarily resolved the situation of the bad notes being played. But you've also lost the second-violin player! What if it were possible to somehow restore the sheet music to this musician? What if it were possible to project the correct resonant frequency to whatever part of the body was vibrating out of ease and out of harmony—and put it back in tune?

The very basis of sound healing is simply the concept that everything is in a state of vibration. Almost every modality utilizes this approach—enhancing the correct resonant frequency of a part of the physical, emotional, mental, or spiritual body. It's important for us to come to this understanding because it demonstrates the power of sound to heal and transform.

Sound for Transformation

Most people think of sound simply as a vibrational energy that enters our ears, goes into our brains, and affects our nervous system. This is true—our heart rate, respiration, and brain waves are all affected by sounds that we hear. But sound is much more.

Sound is an amazing tool for transformation. It has the ability to take that which is vibrating out of ease and put it back *into* ease, balance, and harmony. This can include not only our physical bodies, but also our emotional, mental, and spiritual ones. In addition, sound can affect, alter, and enhance our consciousness. It has the power to actually shift our overall vibratory rate, causing imbalances and disharmonious vibrations to drop away.

An article titled "Sound Is Shaped Into a Dazzling New Tool With Many Uses" in the *New York Times* Science section states: "The beams [of sound] can make, break or rearrange molecules . . . and even levitate objects . . ."

What does the above statement tell us? For one thing, it says that sound is such a powerful energy that it has the ability to affect our cells. It can repattern molecules! It can even change our DNA.

Gregg Braden's discovery that the Tetragrammaton could be translated into our genetic code as the phrase "God/Eternal within the body" demonstrated a remarkable resonance of יהוה within our DNA. From my perspective, listening to the Divine Name allows an amplification of this energy to occur. Learning to intone it as a self-created sound may do even more, enabling extraordinary evolutionary activation of our DNA, perhaps allowing the manifestation of miraculous gifts—what the Hindus called *siddhis*. These are exceptional abilities—which include levitation, telepathy, and much more—that assist in personal and planetary healing. Such abilities have been described in various sacred texts. Could the sounding of the Divine Name facilitate this?

In order for us to understand the true power of sound to heal and transform, it's necessary to examine the concept of sacred sound.

What Is Sacred Sound?

Conceptually, all sound is sacred since it's an aspect of the Creator being. If, as our sacred texts indicate, the original source of creation is sound, and this original sound was that of God, then *all* sound is of God and therefore sacred. Conceptually, this may be correct. However, many theologians and philosophers would probably suggest differently. It's easy to find the sacred in the chanting of Gregorian monks or other liturgical singing, but what about the roaring of a lawn mower or the screaming of a car alarm? Many would find these sounds less than Divine.

In his book *The Magic of Tone and the Art of Music,* noted philosopher and musician Dane Rudhyar pointed out that there is sacred sound, and there is mundane sound. The difference between the two lies in the intent. As an example, the clattering of pots and pans is usually considered a mundane sound, unless it's made with a specific intent—such as healing. For most, the sounds of pots and pans being used for cooking and then being cleaned are at best an annoyance and at worst a disturbance. However, I've heard the banging of pans utilized by shamans of far-off lands for healing purposes, and in those instances these sounds are transformed from the mundane to the sacred. The reason for this is *intent.*

Intention: The Missing Link

To me, *sacred* sound occurs when a sound is encoded with the intention of a positive outcome and beneficial results, such as healing. Oftentimes these intentions are for communion and guidance from higher sources—in other words, prayer.

This recognition of the power of our intent wasn't something I immediately arrived at during my initial study of sound healing. Rather, it occurred in a lightning flash of realization after years of research. But when it did so, the experience changed my understanding of sound and its power to heal and transform.

It was the late 1980s, and I was working on my first book. I'd already received a master's degree from Lesley University, where for several years I'd researched the uses of sound and music for healing. I was taking this material, collecting all the data I'd received, and shaping it into what I perceived would be my grand opus—a monumental manuscript of earth-shattering import.

There was a pile of papers—several hundred pages at least—that I was sorting through to find some sort of common thread for the book I was working on. This assemblage of papers was the result of all the research I'd been conducting with regard to different systems that used sound for healing. I'd realized the power of sound as an extraordinary form of energy for putting that which was out of balance back into balance. The theory behind how and why sound worked made sense. Except for one thing. . . .

In front of me were hundreds of pages' worth of papers with systems of sound healing that had been used by various teachers, scientists, and healers throughout the world. It may have been one of the most thorough and extensive collections available at the time. The trouble was that few, if any, of the various sources were in agreement with each other over the different sounds to use. There was virtually no concordance or coherence among them.

I had systems of frequencies, tones, mantras, and intervals for use on the physical body: for the various organs and systems; for the subtle anatomy; for the chakras, the acupuncture meridians, the etheric fields. I had sounds for virtually every condition imaginable, and then some. But they were all different and didn't concur. Yet they all had resulted in various degrees of healing for the individual.

Scientist A would use frequency A to treat an ailment. Scientist B would use frequency B to treat the same ailment. (Weren't these people talking to each other and comparing notes?) Spiritual Master X would use mantra X to resonate a certain chakra. Spiritual Master Y would use mantra Y to resonate the same chakra. Or one would use the same mantra for a different chakra. It didn't make sense. Nothing lined up.

I remember sitting in front of my computer (this was so long ago that I was using DOS) in a state of intellectual angst. I kept thinking, *How can this be possible?* There had to be some sort of unified theory that would tie this all together, but I couldn't see it at the time.

I believed there was validity in all of the different sounds that these various people were reporting that they were able to successfully use. Yet, if there was the concept of resonant-frequency healing, and all these different people were utilizing different sounds, how could this be? There had to be something more.

Frequency + Intent

I was holding my head in my hands, trying to understand what was going on, when I heard an inner voice say: *It is not only the frequency of the sound that creates the healing; it is also the intention of the person making the sound.* Then I typed out the formula *Frequency + Intent = Healing,* and suddenly everything made sense. "Frequency" was a reference to the actual sound being created. "Intent" was the energy or the consciousness behind the sound and encoded upon it. "Healing" was the desired outcome of the sound. This realization of the importance of intent in conjunction with sound was a truly transformational experience for me.

Frequency + Intent = Healing. It's my "grand theory" of sound, unifying all the variances within the arena. More than 25 years later, it's still as significant and valid as the day I received it. The concept that the actual physical sound, coupled with the energy encoded upon it, creates the *effect* of the sound continues to resonate with me.

Whenever I discuss and teach the meaning of intent and its relationship to "frequency," it's never merely as a mental construct, but something much greater, coming from both the heart and the mind. An entry for *intention* from *Merriam-Webster's Collegiate Dictionary* is "the object for which a prayer, mass, or pious act is offered." This definition has always seemed most relevant—particularly as the power of intent comes more and more into our consciousness.

The Power of Intent

One of the most profound demonstrations of the power of intent can be found in the work of Japanese scientist Masaru Emoto. Emoto began experimenting with water, collecting samples from throughout the world, which he would then freeze and photograph using a special dark-field microscope.

His first photos showed that natural water such as that from a healthy spring would create an image that looked very much like a snowflake. Polluted water, in contrast, created an image that resembled mud. He then began experiments using different sounds to see their effects upon water. Certain music, such as classical and New Age, created extraordinary geometric snowflake-like images, while other genres—violent heavy metal, for instance—created mudlike images.

Emoto's experimentation continued, this time by simply tapping words on bottles of distilled water to see what would happen. The results were startling. When the water crystals were photographed, words such as *Thank You!* created the snowflake shapes. Other words such as *You make me sick!* created mud. These experiments demonstrate the power of intention or consciousness to affect physical matter.

For me, the most dramatic demonstration of Emoto's work involved polluted water from the Fujiwara Dam in Japan. This water, when first photographed, looked like mud. It was then chanted over by a monk reciting a Buddhist prayer. When it was photographed again, it resembled a snowflake!

These photos clearly showed the power of Frequency + Intent to affect the physical structure of water, which composes at least 75 percent of our bodies. If a chanting priest can change the mudlike vibrations of polluted water into the snowflake-like vibrations of clean water, we really should begin to realize the power of sound and consciousness to heal not only our physical bodies, but this entire planet.

These two photographs by Emoto (which are reproduced in my book *The 7 Secrets of Sound Healing*) affected me deeply. It was stunning proof, not only of the power of intentionalized sound to create change, but also the power of vocalized prayer.

Sound and Prayer

When we encode a sound with energy such as prayer and intent, we magnify its effect. And at the same time we magnify the *prayer's* effect. Sound amplifies and enhances prayer. Sound empowers prayer. It is not by coincidence that the majority of the prayer on this planet is vocalized in some manner, whether through singing, chanting, or oral recitation.

Why does sound have the ability to enhance prayer? There are many possible answers. One may be that it helps focus our thoughts and feelings when we vocalize a prayer. When reciting in silence, the person praying can easily get distracted by other thoughts. Chanting the prayers aloud seems to help focus our attention on our *intention*. This is but one reason why sound heightens our consciousness during prayer, enhancing the outcome that manifests.

A more esoteric but equally important reason may be that prayer is a sonic offering to the Divine—an offering more precious than incense, candles, or anything else. In many spiritual texts and illustrations from throughout the world, the Creator is surrounded by celestial beings who are chanting sacred sounds—offering sonics to the Creator—such as the vision from Isaiah 6:2–3 of the angels surrounding God, singing Divine tones. These sacred sounds, including those created by you and me, may produce a deep and profound resonance for all.

Prayer as Heart-Centered Feeling

Gregg Braden's work with the power of prayer is the basis of *The Isaiah Effect: Decoding the Lost Science of Prayer and Prophecy,* as well as many of his other books and teachings. Perhaps the most important aspect of this work involves a very simple yet extremely important and profound aspect of prayer: that it is a heartfelt phenomenon.

While many may perceive prayer as an appeal to higher spiritual forces in order to request something, this petition, coming from a condition of need, is oftentimes unsuccessful. The true power of prayer lies in our being in a state of appreciation and thankfulness while we're praying. This occurs when our thoughts and emotions combine to create a heart-centered feeling that focuses on our appreciation, as though the outcome we desire has already happened. Rather than "asking" for something, we manifest the greatest effect of prayer when we feel that what we're requesting has actually occurred; when we feel this in our hearts and we know that it is real.

For the most effective prayer and manifestation to take place, you must "give thanks" for what you're praying for, as if it is already a fact. This "attitude of gratitude," the heart-centered feeling of appreciation, is perhaps the single most important aspect of prayer and the efficacy of intent.

This information stems from material Gregg uncovered in ancient and arcane spiritual texts that dealt with this subject, as well as the latest scientific knowledge quantum physics provides about the nature of the universe. Both the ancient masters and our greatest scientists agree—we are all interconnected in a universal field of energy. This collective field of consciousness has no separation in terms of time or space—it is infinite—and it is influenced by our beliefs and feelings: by our intent. The most powerful way to affect this field is with the intention of love!

Technology and Technique

In Gregg's work, he has shared that when the actual mechanism of a miracle is understood, it then becomes a technology.

For many, the terms *technology* and *technique* mean the same thing. For our purposes, I differentiate between them in this way:

technology is the knowledge; technique is the application and use of this knowledge.

The power of encoding our intent—our consciousness, feelings, and prayers—upon a sound in order to influence and manifest change in the field of consciousness can be considered a miracle. And our knowledge of how to do this may be considered a form of *technology.* Perhaps the greatest sound that may be utilized to manifest change is the Divine Name. Using it in this manner has the potential to transform the world. We will revisit this purpose at the end of this book.

As we'll discover, we have an extraordinary heartfelt *technique* that gives us the ability to deliver and manifest the power of sound and prayer—a limitless source of energy from the Divine that allows us to create positive shifts toward Global Harmonization. Through the projection of the consciousness of heart-centered prayer on the sounding of the Divine Name, it is possible for Tikkun Olam—the mending of the world—to occur.

Let us now continue with our exploration of the power of self-created sound to effect change on both a personal and planetary level.

Chapter Five

Sounds
of Power

Undoubtedly the most powerful, and certainly the most ancient, instrument of sound to heal and transform is the human voice. Since prehistoric times, humans have used their voices for various types of prayer, from activities such as chanting for the growth of crops, to toning in order to resonate with the Divine. This power of the human voice is particularly effective with regard to projecting and encoding intent, enhancing sacred sound.

Mantras: Universal Sounds of Power

The sounding of a particular spiritual name, word, or phrase to create healing and transformation is found throughout the world. Most frequently, these sounds of power are referred to as *mantras*. The word *mantra* is Sanskrit and translates as "the thought that liberates and protects." Mantras are sounds or words that when recited (either aloud or silently) have the ability to alter the consciousness of the reciter. In the Hindu and Tibetan traditions, the ultimate aim is to unite the reciter with a particular deity or force. Different mantras have different purposes, which will be discussed later.

Despite the Sanskrit origins of the word *mantra,* sounds of power are found in religious and spiritual traditions throughout the planet. There is virtually no place on Earth where the use of self-created sacred sounds doesn't occur.

Anytime a sound or word is repetitively used, it can be considered a mantra, whether it is an *om, shalom, Allah, Ave Maria, alleluia,* or *amen.* Vowel sounds are thought of as sacred and can, of course, be considered mantras. In fact, the Divine Name can be regarded as a mantra, as can the individual letters found within it—יהוה.

How Mantras Work on the Physical

There is much varied speculation on how and why mantras work. I believe a combination of different elements contributes to the power of mantras. Some of these are mundane and physical. Others are esoteric and spiritual. Together, these elements create sounds of power.

On a physical level, chanting a mantra in a slow manner causes the nervous system—including our heart rate, respiration, and brain waves—to attune and entrain with the rhythm of the chant. This alone is quite powerful, because as we slow down our bodily rhythms, we begin to sink into deeper states of consciousness. The result is a decrease in blood pressure, among other effects. When this occurs, we calm ourselves, creating *the relaxation response,* a term used by Herbert Benson, M.D., in his book of the same name.

In addition, different neurochemicals and hormones such as endorphins, those naturally created opiates, are produced in our bodies when these self-created sounds of power are chanted. It has also been found that when we do this activity with other people, the neurotransmitter *oxytocin,* the trust hormone, is released. Sounding together creates trust, breaking down barriers of separation that may have previously existed. No wonder we feel good afterward.

In his book *Self-Healing: Powerful Techniques,* Ranjie N. Singh, Ph.D., describes his discovery that different mantras and self-created sounds trigger the release of *melatonin,* a hormone primarily produced in the brain that has many purposes, including regulating our sleep cycle, and which is now being used experimentally to shrink tumors. Recent research suggests that melatonin may also be useful as an antidepressant.

Nitric oxide (NO) is a powerful molecule that is associated with the healing process, including boosting the immune system and increasing vascular flow. It has been found that NO is activated in conjunction with specific sounds—particularly through the production of certain self-created sounds such as humming. It may be that the acoustic vibrations of our own sounds can resonate our internal organs and cause NO to be released. The work of Bruce Lipton, Ph.D., the author of *The Biology of Belief,* has shown how our cells and DNA respond to various environmental stimuli—particularly sound. As previously mentioned, the Divine Name may be a sound that resonates deeply with our DNA.

I have little doubt that with continued research, there will be more scientific data related to why chanting mantras has beneficial physiological effects upon the chanter. Currently, these specific effects include:

- Increased oxygen in the cells
- Lowered blood pressure and heart rate

- Increased lymphatic circulation
- Elevated levels of melatonin
- Reduced levels of stress-related hormones
- Release of endorphins—self-created opiates that work as "natural pain relievers"
- Boosted production of *interleukin-l,* a protein associated with blood production
- Increased levels of nitric oxide (NO), a molecule associated with the promotion of healing
- Release of oxytocin, the "trust" hormone

Sounding sacred tones and mantras affects the physical body, including our nervous system, our cells, our molecules, and even our DNA. In addition, sound can resonate and affect our chakras and related aspects of our subtle anatomy. The power of sound to influence us should not be underestimated.

An Extraordinary Experience

After three decades in this field, I've had many extraordinary experiences as a result of working with sacred sound. Some of these include witnessing spontaneous healings and other miraculous events. In addition, I've heard enough anecdotal stories about the healing and transformational power of sound from other people to fill a book. Despite all these extraordinary encounters in the field of sound, one personal story particularly stands out, and I'd like to share it with you. It really demonstrates an aspect of sound that was quite beyond the realm of anything I could have anticipated, and continues to astound me to this day.

In 1987, an event took place that many believe created an important and powerful shift in planetary consciousness called the *Harmonic Convergence*. It was a time when like-minded individuals throughout the world meditated and chanted together in order to usher in a new era of peace and harmony. The specific dates for this were August 16 and 17. The Harmonic Convergence was said to open a gateway of consciousness that would culminate in major transformation on December 21, 2012.

I found myself in Mexico during this time of the Harmonic Convergence. First, I journeyed to legendary Tule Tree, where Mayan prophecies had foretold that Quetzalcoatl, the plumed serpent god, would emerge and bring forth a new epoch of consciousness on the planet. Next, I immediately traveled to Palenque, where the Mayans had built a city with structures reminiscent of ancient Egypt.

Late one night a guide took five of my traveling companions and me on a special tour of Palenque. He told us he would share a journey through this site that we wouldn't otherwise experience. Indeed, he was correct.

At one point in our tour, our guide led us into a temple that had been closed to the public. Using a flashlight, he took us to a chamber on a subterranean level. He and I had spoken briefly about my interest in sound. Once the entire group was in this ancient room, our guide pointed toward the doorway of the chamber and said: "Make sound here!" Then he turned off his flashlight.

I'd never before been in such total darkness. There was no light anywhere.

"Make sound," he urged.

"Sure," I replied. Then I began to tone some vowel sounds, complete with harmonics. To my utter amazement, the room started to become illuminated. Somehow, I'd been able to create light—perhaps fields of it—through the harmonically related sound of the vowels. It wasn't like the illumination from a flashlight or some outside source, but rather, it was more subtle.

The room literally began to get brighter. I could see the outlines and figures of the people there. Everyone was aware of this, and after I stopped toning, the room was filled with the exclamations of the others, who had also experienced this light, which was now fading. Then our guide turned his flashlight back on, and we continued on our tour.

Since that time, I've investigated explanations from both the scientific and the spiritual communities. I've speculated on many different possibilities for what occurred, but there simply is no single explanation that encompasses all the aspects of this phenomenon. It was real. There were witnesses. And it is true. After a while, I cease to explain, and simply accept what is.

Mantras as Cosmic Tuning Forks

I have extensive experience exploring and working with sacred sounds from many different traditions, chanting and toning them for hours. I've sounded them audibly. I've sounded them inaudibly. I've done so lying down. I've done so sitting up. Eyes open. Eyes closed. Visualizing a deity. Visualizing a color. Projecting an intent. *Not* projecting an intent. I've even practiced with a blank mind, with no visualization or thoughts at all. I've experimented with almost every imaginable variation with respect to these Divine names, using myself as the laboratory.

I acknowledge that there are differences in how one actually vocalizes the sound that can influence its physiological effect. However, more important, I acknowledge that each of these sounds of power is unique. They each seem to have a very specific energy that remains constant regardless of the method of sounding. Here is an explanation of why this may occur, according to Swami Vishnu-Devananda in *Meditation and Mantras:*

Everything in the universe vibrates on specific wavelengths. These wavelengths can be manipulated. For example, when its pitch is created high enough, a violin note can shatter glass. The various mantras, although equally efficient, vibrate on different wavelengths.

Thus, by repeating a mantra over and over, individuals are able to attune their own vibrational frequencies with the energy of this sound of power. Ultimately this activity will cause them to resonate with a particular deity or force toward which the mantra is geared. It's almost as though mantras are sonic formulas that, once put together, create a waveform of sonic energy that is specific to them, just as chemical formulas can create particular compounds through the addition of different substances. By resonating with that deity or force, one *attunes* with it. Thus, the use of these sounds of power can cause union with gods and goddesses, allowing the attainment of enlightenment or the achievement of great feats. The powers and abilities that can be obtained or tapped into through the use of mantras are potentially limitless.

I've found that a mantra works almost as a kind of cosmic "god" sound, where the reciter becomes like a celestial tuning fork that vibrates and attracts the energy of whatever or whomever one is sounding *to.* I've literally felt the Divine energy of different mantras come into my body, affecting me on a physical, emotional, mental, and spiritual level. I know that people in my workshops have also experienced this.

Most frequently in my workshops, we have worked with benevolent energies from the Hindu, Tibetan, Hebrew, Islamic, and Christian traditions. I'm always very aware of what the different attributes of a mantra are before I share it with anyone else. This is based upon my own research and experimentation. Thus, I'm sure about the effects of a particular sound before I introduce it to the participants.

In groups, we will often chant a mantra for about a half hour or more. The results are mind-altering. People report profound experiences—deep meditations and even deeper inner journeys. Above all, there have often been reports of encounters with the deity that represented the energy of the mantra. If, for example, it is a Tibetan mantra for compassion that invokes the Buddha of Compassion, called *Avalokiteshvara,* people may encounter this being during the sounding or in the meditation that follows. Or they may encounter someone or something else (it could, for instance, be another celestial being or even an animal) in their psyches that represents the energy of compassion. It's quite extraordinary and presents more validation of the power of mantra.

Vocalization + Visualization

While sounds of power seem to be spiritually encoded with specific sacred energy, it seems that we as reciters can enhance this energy even more through our understanding of the mantra, the energy that we're anticipating, and the visualization we're doing. Many years ago, when I initially created the formula *Frequency + Intent = Healing,* another formula also manifested. It was very similar to the first one, but seemed to have more relevance to the sounding of mantras: *Vocalization + Visualization = Manifestation.* By "visualization," like "intent," I was not simply referring to a mental-plane construct, but in addition, a heartfelt energy. Thus, when we chant the mantra of compassion, "Om Mani Padme Hum," we not only visualize the Buddha of Compassion, but also feel the energy of compassion at the same time.

I was recently talking with Kailash, the author of *Following Sound into Silence,* a book that focuses upon the power of Hindu and Tibetan mantras. We had similar understandings of the subject, and thus I asked him a question I'd personally meditated upon for many years: if each of the mantras has a specific energy or deity associated with it, did it matter how much people understood its meaning while chanting it, as well as using visualizations of the deity? In other words, how much of the mantra was based upon the actual energy encoded on it, and how much was based upon people's understanding of and belief in it?

Increasing the Power

We both agreed upon the answer: the mantra by itself was powerful. However, with understanding, feeling, and visualization, the power was greatly amplified and enhanced. Thus, the importance of our consciousness as it relates to a sound—even one that is considered by itself to be sacred—shouldn't be undervalued. There is a feedback loop that occurs when we make sound—it affects us, and we affect it. Our resonance with it—from a physical, emotional, mental, and spiritual level—truly influences its power and energy. This is important for us to understand *whenever* we make sound, and in particular when we make sacred sound.

The power of these sacred sounds is much greater, and of greater significance, than we can currently completely understand. Through honoring the extraordinary knowledge of ancient spiritual masters, coupled with the modern wisdom of our quantum physicists, we can acknowledge the amazing ability of mantras and other sacred sounds to heal and transform. While we're still in the very early stages of being able to grasp the totality of the wonders and powers of sacred sound, the importance of our understanding of intent, visualization, and feeling with respect to sound, and our application of these ideas, cannot be overstated.

As I've said before, in my experience, throughout the many years I've used the various sounds of power from the numerous traditions I've encountered, the Divine Name is the most exceptional. This also seems to be true for others who have vocalized it. For many, having knowledge of mantras, and particularly that of the Divine Name, is helpful in understanding the power and majesty of the personal name of God.

Now, let us move on to what I consider to be the most universal sounds of power on this planet—the vowels.

Chapter Six

Vowels
and
Harmonics

$\mathcal{M}$y life has been dedicated to raising awareness of the healing and transformational uses of sound and music. If I were asked for the single *most* transformational sound experience I've had, it would undoubtedly be with the use of vowel sounds. Contained within these phonemes (bits of sound) are worlds, perhaps even galaxies or universes, of sonic energy and expression . . . of resonance and transformation. My initial discovery of the Divine Name was the direct result of sounding the vowels in a specific sequence.

Vowels are universal. They're found in every language and every tradition. If someone from one country sounds forth a vowel with a specific intent, it will sound the same and have the same feeling as it would for someone from another country sounding the same vowel with the same intent. With vowels there is no language barrier. It is instant communication.

The Tower of Babel

In the Old Testament is the story of the Tower of Babel—in which humans tried to build a literal stairway to heaven. At the time, they were all able to communicate with each other while doing this project, indicating that there was a universal language. However, as a result of their arrogance and pride, God caused them to speak different languages so they would be unable to understand each other. All that would have been necessary would have been to add the consonants in different sequences in order to create confusion in the different languages that resulted. This is why many perceive vowels as being the sounds that unite, while consonants are the sounds that divide.

Vowels Are Sacred

Few people realize that in many traditions, vowels are considered sacred. I've been involved with many different esoteric approaches to sound, and most of them involve the use of vowel sounds. These traditions include the Enochi from Japan, Tibetan Buddhists, Islamic Sufis, Surat Shabd yoga practitioners, the Native American medicine people, and those of many other indigenous cultures. Shamans, mystics, and sound healers from throughout the world understand the power and importance of vowels. Many spiritual practitioners from different traditions understand and utilize combinations of different vowels to create the sacred sound of the Divine. I used to think of these sounds as being non-denominational, meaning that they aren't formally aligned with any religious denomination. Now, in addition, I consider them to be *trans*-denominational: they transcend all denominations and have the capacity to bring all faiths together.

I had the opportunity to speak with Abd'El Hakim Awyan, a noted archaeologist and mystical teacher from an Egyptian tradition so ancient that he referred to himself as a Khemitologist (Khemit is the name of the land before it was renamed Egypt by the Greeks). We spoke of the extraordinary power of sacred vowels to heal and transform.

Along with Egypt, many of the ancient mystery schools, including those of Greece, had knowledge of the use of sacred vowel sounds to heal and transform. According to Donald Beaman, the author of *The Tarot of Saqqara,* the Gnostics, a very early Christian sect, sounded the name of God as *IAO.*

Perhaps nowhere is the power of vowels more thoroughly acknowledged than in the Kabbalistic tradition. Many Kabbalistic mystics believe that the vowels were the sounds of the heavens. The consonants were the sounds of the earth. Together, they made for communication. William Gray, in his seminal Kabbalistic work *The Talking Tree,* writes: "The vowels were originally very special sonics indeed, being mostly used for 'God-names' and other sacred purposes." Gray further states that the chanting of particular vowel sounds has the ability to connect the chanter with the energies of the Divine.

Joscelyn Godwin, in *The Mystery of the Seven Vowels,* tells us that this understanding of the power and sacred energy of the vowels is said to have been known by the Egyptians, who then passed this knowledge on to the Greeks. He states that Nicomachus of Gerasa around the 1st century A.D. described a use of toning the seven sacred vowel sounds in order to act as "the primary sounds emitted by the seven heavenly bodies."

Toning

In order to truly explore the subject of vowel sounds, we need to examine the area of sound known as *toning,* a term first attributed to Laurel Elizabeth Keyes, whose classic book *Toning: The Creative Power of the Voice* was initially published in the 1970s. Keyes began using this term in the '60s to describe the use of vocally created sounds as a therapeutic tool. She relied heavily on extended vowel sounds for this. In her book, she wrote: "Toning is an ancient method of healing . . . the idea is simply to restore people to their harmonic patterns."

Don G. Campbell, who has recently released an updated version of Keyes's classic text, stated in his own book on the subject, *The Roar of Silence:* "'Toning' is defined in this book as the conscious elongation of a sound using the breath and voice."

Laeh Maggie Garfield, in *Sound Medicine,* described toning as: "a system of healing that utilized vowel sounds to alter vibrations in every molecule and cell of the body." As previously mentioned, according to a *New York Times* article, sound does indeed seem to have the ability to rearrange molecular structure.

John Beaulieu in *Music and Sound in the Healing Arts* wrote: "Toning is the process of making vocal sounds for the purpose of balance." He adds that "toning sounds are sounds of expression and do not have a precise meaning." This information suggests that *because* vowels do not have a precise meaning, we don't have to engage our minds with the content and context of the sound.

Toning a sound for self-resonance and healing isn't singing. It's something everyone can learn to do. With toning, I'm not talking about getting up in front of people and belting out "Strangers in the Night" or some other song. That's entertainment. Singing songs is performance art, not toning.

Toning isn't entertainment. It's *entrainment,* a scientific term for using sound for frequency shifting—using self-created tones to change and balance yourself. With toning, there is no need to judge yourself on whether you're making the "right" sound or a "good" sound. Any tone that you make as long as it feels comfortable for you is a right and a good one.

Whether you realize it or not, you've been toning all your life. Just think about what happens when you're in pain—you moan and groan. Mostly likely, these sounds are an elongated "Aaahhhh" or "Oooohhhh." These are part of the body's natural response dealing with pain and assisting in creating balance. If you're skeptical, next time you hit the funny bone of your elbow, don't make a sound and see what happens. No doubt it will hurt more. Or better yet, if you're in pain and you've been resisting the urge to make a sound, go for it. It will help.

No one knows exactly *why* this type of toning helps, but it does work. One school of thought posits that making sounds creates a distraction for the mind, helping relieve the pain. Others feel that when making the sound, we may actually be resonating the part of the body that is giving us pain, helping heal it and put it into balance. As mentioned in the previous chapter, some researchers suggest that such sounds may trigger endorphins, naturally occurring opiates that alleviate pain. Still others propose that our self-created sounds cause the release of nitric oxide, a molecule that enhances the healing process. There are myriad explanations still under investigation.

Vowel Sounds

Why vowel sounds? One explanation may simply be that vowel sounds are nonverbal—unlike words, they're expressions that usually have no meaning (they often convey feeling and can be easily encoded with intent). In addition, when you pronounce an elongated vowel, there is no constriction in your breath and sound. In fact, if you want to lengthen a word, you usually have to elongate the vowel sounds in order to do so. Most consonants are sharp and short. Some are longer, but few have the elongated power of the vowels, which are great for making extended vocal sounds. They're also excellent for creating resonance in the body.

Out of all the letters in our alphabet, there seems to be something special about the vowels that is universally understood. When sounded, they convey particular and specific feelings. An

"Ah" intoned as a loving sound in Japan or India will be perceived the same as an "Ah" intoned as a loving sound in Kenya, England, or Brazil. Acknowledgment of the sacredness of vowels transcends different religions and spiritual groups. These sounds seem to be acknowledged by all as being sacred and special. Perhaps the reason why has to do with harmonics.

Harmonics

Harmonics are one of the most mysterious and important aspects of sound. From my perspective, this subject is so important that I've written an entire book, *Healing Sounds: The Power of Harmonics,* dedicated to it.

Simply put, harmonics are the colors of sound. Have you ever placed a prism in sunlight and seen how the light goes in one side, is refracted by the prism, and comes out the other side as all the colors of the rainbow? I'm sure we all have.

Sound is a lot like sunlight going through a prism—it's actually composed of a number of different frequencies that merge together to form what we hear. We often think that sounds are just single-tone frequencies, but they're not. In fact, all naturally occurring sounds are composed of multiple frequencies. These different frequencies are called *harmonics.* They're also known as *overtones,* and the two terms are used interchangeably.

If, for example, we pluck a string on an instrument that is tuned to 100 Hz, the first fundamental frequency that will occur is 100 Hz. The string will be vibrating up and down 100 times per second. However, in addition, it's simultaneously vibrating up and down many more times, generating specific overtones. This is important to understand: the string isn't merely creating one vibration—it's creating multiple vibrations through the harmonics that manifest from it.

The concept of the sounds that occur in nature being composite frequencies can be a real "ear-opener" to those unaware of this phenomenon. Often it leads to a level of deeper listening, with people hearing sounds within sounds—the result of our beginning to perceive overtones.

Harmonics in Nature

This mathematical multiplication that applies to harmonics can be observed throughout nature. In fact, harmonics corresponds to an underlying framework existing in chemistry, physics, crystallography, astronomy, architecture, spectroanalysis, botany, and the other nature sciences. The relationship expressed in the periodic table of elements resembles the overtone structure in music, as does that of the orbital distances of the planets.

With the preceding example of the fundamental frequency vibrating at 100 Hz, the first overtone that occurs is vibrating twice as fast, at 200 Hz (100 × 2 = 200). The next overtone that occurs is vibrating at three times the speed of that first, fundamental frequency—at 300 Hz. The next overtone vibrates four times as fast. And so on.

The example of 100 Hz as the fundamental frequency was used in order to easily understand that harmonics are multiples of a given frequency, going twice as fast, three times as fast, and so on. This "multiples" phenomenon of harmonics applies to any fundamental frequency, whether it be 423 Hz or 865 Hz or whatever. I simply used 100 Hz because the numbers were easy to follow.

Conceptually at least, harmonics go on forever, continuing to multiply themselves as they manifest. However, we're most sensitive to the first 15 harmonics—those that are usually the most audible.

Formants

Harmonics are normally a part of the sonic spectrum, incorporated into the sounds we're hearing, whether they're from a voice, an instrument, or nature. However, not all harmonics are created equal. Some are louder than others. While they do indeed vibrate simultaneously, certain ones are the most audible and pronounced. These are called *formants*.

Formants are the loudest harmonics that we hear. They're responsible for why things sound the way they do. Harmonics are, as I said before, the colors of sound. They are responsible for the individual timbre (pronounced *tam-ber*), or tone color, of whatever we're hearing. Different instruments, as well as our voices, have different harmonics that are most perceptible—different formants that make these instruments sound unique and individual.

These most audible harmonics are responsible for why we can distinguish between different instruments. Harmonics are vitally important in sound because they determine the unique characteristics of each sound we hear. An experiment was done in a sound laboratory where all the harmonics were removed from various instruments, and it was impossible to distinguish between them. Normally, we can easily tell the difference between a trumpet, violin, and flute.

Harmonics are also responsible for why our voices sound the way they do. It is said that every voice is unique—that no two are exactly alike—somewhat like our fingerprints. This is mainly because of the formants—the most audible harmonics in our voice. There is very complicated scientific machinery that can track this exactly for each individual. Suffice it to say that each person's voice has many formants that have different levels of volume. The potential is endless, which is why our individual voices are unique.

Vocal Harmonics

As noted, overtones occur simultaneously, and normally we aren't able to distinguish them individually. However, trained musicians can usually learn to quiet and suppress the fundamental frequency, playing specific overtones on their instruments. This is also true with certain vocalists who have learned a technique to individually generate harmonics while they sound a fundamental frequency.

It's possible to learn how to bring out the various harmonics of a tone using specific vocal techniques so that they're audible and noticeable. These vocal harmonics can be quite striking to listen to. Sometimes they sound like a ghost voice, a flute, or a bagpipe. Sometimes they sound like a bell, whistle, or buzzing. Vocal harmonics can be transformational to create and mysterious to hear. A well-trained harmonic singer can produce the first 15 harmonics quite audibly.

Many of the ancient mystery schools, in Egypt and other places, probably utilized vocal harmonics as part of their spiritual and transformational practices. While most of these mystical sound practices have been lost, there still exist several different traditions that have learned to consciously manipulate vocal sounds so that the overtones they create are noticeably audible above the fundamental tone. In Tibet, certain monks have gained the ability to create a very "deep voice" or "growl tone" while generating specific overtones. In Mongolia and the Tuva Republic, a different form of creating vocal harmonics, called *hoomi,* or "throat singing," has been developed. Both the Tibetan and the Mongolian/Tuvan techniques require much practice and can be extremely difficult for most Westerners.

Today, in the West, there has emerged a new form of vocal harmonics used as an artistic form and/or spiritual practice. I call this the "nouvo-European" technique. The creation of these vocal harmonics differs from those of Tibet and other Eastern locales in that this newer technique produces ones that are easy to learn. This technique also doesn't require exotic vocal contortions, which can sometimes be difficult on the vocal cords. Most noticeably, the creation of vocal harmonics relies heavily on using the vowel sounds sung in an ordinary voice.

How do the vowel sounds generate vocal harmonics? The answer is simple—through the specific harmonics that are associated with each and every one. Each vowel's unique structure of formants is what makes it sound distinct from another. Harmonics are in fact being created all the time, even when we're speaking. While they may not be audible during speech, they are there.

Through toning extended vowel sounds, it's quite easy to begin to hear "sounds within sounds" in the vowels that are created. These are, of course, harmonics. As I mentioned, every vowel sound has specific harmonics that are produced. Thus, through the use of vowels, we can easily learn to generate harmonics.

The Language of the Birds

In many legends and myths, there are stories of a language—a harmonically related tongue—through which all people and all creatures could communicate. It has been called "the language of the birds" or "the language of light." Perhaps through toning the vowel sounds and their corresponding vocal harmonics, we're rediscovering this universal language. And perhaps the Divine Name is a key to this.

There's one more thing I'd like to share, which I trust will bring this chapter and its relationship to the rest of the book together. But first, I'd like to summarize the information covered so far:

- Toning is the extended sounding of vowels.

- Vowels are considered sacred in many traditions.

- Harmonics are geometric multiples of a fundamental sound that naturally occur whenever the sound is created.

- Different "stressed" harmonics, called *formants,* are responsible for the timbre (or tonal color) of different instruments, as well as our voices.

- Each vowel sound has a different set of harmonics that is heard when it is toned.

The Divine Name as Vowels

With this in mind, I remind you of what I wrote earlier in this book: When I followed the instructions on how to intone the Divine Name that I was given upon waking from my dream state, the sound was composed exclusively of vowels. This particular set of vowels when vocalized sounded very much like "Yahweh" (יהוה, YHVH)—the Divine Name. These vowels first created a descending series of harmonics (that is, they went down), and then an ascending (upward) series. The resonance of these harmonics related to different parts of my body, as well as the subtle energy centers called chakras: The higher harmonics resonated the top of my head and its associated chakras. The lower harmonics resonated the lower parts of my body and *their* associated chakras.

When I sounded these vowels together, the energy went from the top of my head to the base of my trunk and then back out the top of my head. The effect of sounding these vowels in this manner was profound—the most powerful sound experience I'd ever had.

In the next chapter, we'll examine the chakras and the use of vowel sounds to resonate and vibrate these energy centers.

Chapter Seven

The Chakras
and Sound

The previous chapter dealt with the magic and mystery of vowels, including toning, harmonics, formants, and the sacredness of these sounds. It concluded with a statement about the vowel sounds being able to vibrate the energy centers of the body—the chakras.

As previously described, each vowel sound has a particular set of harmonics that resonates most powerfully. Harmonics, in turn, have a quality by which they're able to resonate both the body *and* the chakras, which are composed of subtle energy—vibrations that aren't dense enough to manifest as physical matter.

Spinning Wheels of Light

In the 1980s, during my study at Lesley University, my initial investigation into the area of sound healing was primarily focused on the relationship between sound and the chakras. The word *chakra* is a Sanskrit term meaning "wheel," for that's what these objects look like to those with the ability to see subtle energy. The concept of chakras as energy centers isn't limited to the Eastern traditions of Hinduism and Buddhism, but is found in spiritual and healing paths throughout the world.

Many of the esoteric and occult mystery schools describe these energy centers as "spinning wheels of light." An example of this may be found in the Tree of Life, a Kabbalistic geometric form composed of spheres of light, which many mystics, psychics, and healers have understood to correspond to the chakras. While they are incorporated in many spiritual practices, their existence seems to be based not upon religion, but upon awareness of energy. There is even scientific instrumentation that is beginning to record and validate the chakras.

There are seven main chakras, which are *transduction points*—places where subtle energy from higher realms of vibration begins to grow denser. As the energy from the chakras becomes denser and denser, its vibration continues to slow down as it comes into the body. It next occupies the acupuncture points and meridians. Finally, this energy transduces into the density of the physical body.

The Seven Chakras

There are seven main chakras, seven spinning balls of energy that are located centrally in the front, as well as corresponding to the posterior, of the body. The following is a brief description of the chakras:

- The **1st** or root chakra, located at the base of the spine, is involved with the physical process of elimination and the organs that work with that function. It is the chakra associated with the emotional energy of survival, as well as with grounding to the physical plane.

- The **2nd** or sacral chakra is located about three inches below the navel. This chakra corresponds to sexual energy and the reproductive organs. It is also associated with creativity and our life force.

- The **3rd** or solar-plexus chakra is located at the navel and several inches above. Its energy is associated with digestion and the digestive organs, personal power, and mastery of self.

- The **4th** or heart chakra is located in the center of the chest. On the physical level, it works with the lungs and the heart. On the emotional level, it works with the energy of compassion and love.

- The **5th** or throat chakra is located in the throat area, at the base of the neck. It is the chakra that is involved with the process of communication, speech, and hearing. The ears are associated with this chakra, as well as the vocal apparatus.

- The **6th** or brow chakra is located in the center of the forehead, between and slightly above the eyes. Often called "the third eye," it is associated with imagination and psychic abilities, along with mental activity and brain function.

- The **7th** or crown chakra is located at the top of the head and is related to the induction of spiritual energy into the body. Said to control every aspect of the body and mind, it is associated with full enlightenment and union with God. This chakra is normally not fully opened in most humans, although pictures of saints and other spiritual beings with "halos" are depictions of activated crown chakras.

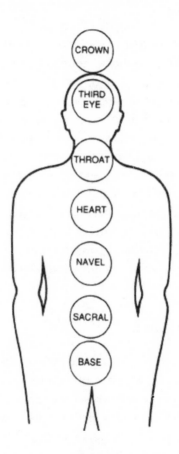

Chakras as Sound

If we understand that everything is vibration and therefore can be conceived of as being sound, this would include our chakras. Our chakras are sound, and their energy can be influenced through the use of other sounds. This was a main area of study for me and the focus of much of my research.

While I was studying at Lesley University, I spent a considerable amount of time researching various ways in which sound could be used to resonate, balance, and otherwise affect the chakras. I discovered and explored many different systems that incorporated frequencies, mantras, intervals, and assorted sounds that all seemed to be effective in terms of influencing the chakras. The most universally effective and powerful chakra-resonating system works with our own voices, utilizing the sacred vowel sounds.

The Chakras and Vowels

It's important to note that while I spent much time researching the work of others who had utilized sound with the chakras, my primary experience with vowel sounds has been simply the result of years and years of experimentation with sound using not only myself, but also hundreds of others in my workshops, as a foundation for my teachings. Once I'd repeatedly experience a phenomenon, I would then share my own findings with other individuals. After enough validation had come through others, I'd eventually begin teaching this information in workshops. This is what occurred with my discovery of the Divine Name.

My Personal Discovery

My personal experience with the Divine Name is an example of one of the most important aspects of learning to use sound—that is, the understanding of the sound itself as being a teacher. The more we practice working with sound, the more we become aware of the feelings and resonances that occur. The more this happens, the greater our understanding—on a deep and personal level—of all that sound has to offer. There is amazing information that it has to teach—we can learn so much simply by experiencing it. When making sound, we go from the realm of theory to that of experience. And once we experience something for ourselves, it becomes real and true, and it can't be denied.

With regard to the system of vowel sounds that I developed, I'd like to acknowledge that the concept of using vowels to resonate the chakras isn't new. Edgar Cayce, the Sleeping Prophet, in one of his readings referred to the priests of ancient Egypt as having knowledge of the use of the seven sacred vowel sounds to resonate their energy centers. In my book *Healing Sounds,* I write about several modern systems of doing so, including those of Kay Gardner and Randall McClellan, in addition to my own.

I refer to the system I developed working with the vowel sounds and chakras as "Vowels as Mantra." My personal discovery involving this occurred on March 21, 1986. I was deep in a sonic meditation on the spring equinox when I "received" this particular system. I wrote it down, experimented more with it, and eventually began teaching it to others.

I'm pleased that while there are other systems that continue to be used, the one I created on that day seems to have become almost universally accepted—to such a degree that I often see it in books with no reference to me . . . or anyone else, for that matter. This system is, for the most part, accepted as fact. Perhaps this is because what I developed is simply most accessible. For whatever reason, I'm grateful that it has been so well received and so frequently utilized.

Scientific Validation of Vowel Resonance

As explained in the previous chapter, there are specific harmonics within each vowel sound. Regardless of the frequency or pitch, a natural resonance with the chakras occurs because of these harmonics in the vowels.

When I created the particular system I call "Vowels as Mantra," I was as much influenced by research in speech pathology as I was by spiritual practices. In speech pathology, I discovered that different vowels naturally seemed to resonate different parts of the body. These parts of the body correlated with the chakras—so that, for example, vowels that naturally resonated in the head region were associated with the third-eye and crown chakras. This very well may be due to the harmonic formants inherent in the specific vowels. Here was validation of a difference in the resonance of the vowel sounds from an entirely different perspective—that of the scientific community.

Chakras and Healing

As suggested in the description of the chakras, there seems to be a major relationship between the chakras and the physical body. Imbalances in the latter can be detected through the former. Healing of the physical occurs much more rapidly when the subtle anatomy—particularly the chakras—is aligned after injury. In addition, very often healers who work with subtle energy can detect imbalances before they manifest in the physical body by feeling them in the chakras. By balancing the chakras, we frequently find that imbalances in the physical body will disappear. In addition, when we do so, we also balance our subtle anatomy.

Thus, we can work with the chakras to put both the physical and subtle bodies back into a state of health and harmony.

In addition, we can work with the chakras as a sort of "preventive medicine"—keeping our chakras balanced and aligned seems to be quite effective in helping us stay healthy and aiding our immune system. Vowel sounds stimulate the endocrine system, such as the pineal, thymus, and adrenal glands. These sounds elicit a physiological response, causing different neurochemicals and hormones to be released. Years of personal experience, as well as recent scientific research, validate this.

Chakras and Consciousness

As we resonate our chakras, balancing and aligning them, we also find that our state of awareness becomes enhanced and our consciousness accelerates. Sounding our chakras with vowels activates higher levels of being, raising our vibratory rate and allowing us to adjust our frequency level. This enables us to create health and harmony within the body, mind, and spirit.

In the next chapter, we'll begin utilizing and putting into practice the information explored thus far. We'll focus on the specific vowel sounds for resonating each of our chakras, learning their particular sequence and assimilating this in order to fully experience their resonance within our own body, mind, and spirit. We'll be combining our understanding of the chakras with our knowledge of the power and sacredness of the vowel sounds.

Part III

Learning to Intone the Divine Name

Chapter Eight

Toning the Chakras

As we've been discovering, vowels are extremely powerful sounds, and our chakras are extremely important aspects of the subtle body. Both are interrelated with the physical body. Sound quite naturally interfaces with our chakras—particularly our own sounds. If there is any experience that can unequivocally demonstrate the power of sound, it is the one in this chapter. As I mentioned in the last chapter, I refer to the ability of our vowels to resonate our chakras as "Vowels as Mantra." I know you will appreciate this exercise to tone the chakras.

The Power of Breath

Before we begin working with our chakras and their associated vowel sounds, there's something I must share with you. It's a very important aspect of sound—the power of breath.

Breath is the essence of life, and it's sacred in many spiritual traditions. In Hinduism, this energy is called *prana*. In the Orient, it's known as *chi* or *ki*. In the Hebrew tradition, one word for breath is *ruach,* which also means "spirit." Wilhelm Reich, Sigmund Freud's disciple, called this energy *orgone* and spent years studying its power. It goes by many different names in the various cultures, countries, and spiritual paths. Still, it is the same energy of breath.

The science of breath has been the subject of many great teachings. Books have been written on this topic, and it's the basis of many esoteric studies, including that of yoga.

Breath is the source of life. It is also the source of *sound*. You can't make sound—at least not any vocally created sound—without breath. Thus, it's important to be sure that you're able to breathe as fully and powerfully as possible before beginning to work with self-created sounds.

What is most important is to focus your awareness on taking as deep a breath as possible. When you breathe deeply down into your lungs and abdomen, you can feel your chest expand, as well as your stomach rise. This is called "diaphragmatic breathing." If you find your rib cage and stomach beginning to expand as you inhale, you're probably breathing in this manner. It allows for the greatest amount of air to enter your body.

Diaphragmatic breathing is very natural. When you watch infants, you'll see that it's what they do. By breathing in this way, you're increasing the supply of oxygen to your bloodstream, and thus giving all the organs of your body more energy. Slow, deep breathing not only oxygenates your body and brain, but it also slows down your heart rate and brain waves, helping induce a state of calm and relaxation. This is excellent for your health.

Here is a simple way to experience diaphragmatic breathing: Lie on the floor, put your hands on your stomach, and take a nice deep breath. . . .

1. Watch as your belly relaxes and rises.

2. Feel your lungs and abdomen expanding as you inhale.

3. Exhale, and feel your stomach relax as the air is pushed out of your lungs.

Do this again and again until it begins to feel natural.

Congratulations! You're now doing diaphragmatic breathing. It's natural and easy, and it can make a tremendous difference in your life, not only affecting the way you create sound, but much more. By bringing in more air as you breathe, you'll be charging yourself with more life energy.

Vowels as Mantra

Next, I'd like to present the "Vowels as Mantra" exercise for toning the chakras, using the power of breath that I introduced in the previous section.

Please be aware that it's important to always be in a place of comfort where you won't be disturbed when working with self-created sounds. And remember to breathe deeply and slowly before, during, and after the sounding. Whenever you're working with your own sound, be sure that what you're creating is gentle and comfortable and not straining your voice in any way. It's not recommended that you make loud sounds during this or any of the other exercises in this book.

Finding Your Pitch

When intoning the vowels for these exercises, you'll want to find a sound—a pitch, note, or key (all three of these terms are basically the same)—that is comfortable for you, in which you don't experience any pain or uneasiness. Creating one is very natural. Simply make a relaxed sound after taking a deep breath. Don't *think* about the pitch. Just make the sound that feels most comfortable—that's usually a good pitch for you.

I have a pretty extensive vocal range after many years of working with sound. However, I often like to make a midrange sound—one that's not too deep and not too high for me. Frequently, I'll find a pitch that's slightly higher than my normal speaking voice. I usually feel it in my throat and chest. Of course, different sounds can resonate different parts of the body, but for the purpose of learning to intone the Divine Name, simply work with whatever pitch feels comfortable for you.

The Instructional CD

Included with this book is an accompanying recording, *The Divine Name Instructional CD,* referred to as the "Instructional CD," which I've created to assist you in learning to sound the Divine Name. This CD is designed to be an interactive companion to the book, and to be used in conjunction with the different exercises that are described. All of the exercises in the following chapters are found on this CD. By listening to these recorded examples, you'll be training your ears, brain, and voice on how these exercises may sound. There will also be material on the CD not found in this book that may be extremely useful in the process of learning to intone the Divine Name.

In addition, there are special sacred sonics on this recording that are encoded at the threshold of our hearing. These sounds include excerpts from *The Divine Name: Sounds of the God Code,* as well as the declarative statement: "Only of Love & Light Through Sound," which is repeated throughout the recording. It is my belief that the inclusion of these encoded sounds will positively affect our consciousness and the resultant impact of *The Divine Name Instructional CD.*

It's now time to begin using this CD as an integral part of the exercises in these pages.

Please listen to Track 1 on the Instructional CD.

Track 1 is an important introduction to the CD, the demonstrated sounds on it, and its relationship with this book. I trust you'll find this track interesting, enjoyable, and helpful to your experience of the exercises.

There are many different ways of toning the chakras—numerous variants that use many different potential notes for each of the vowel sounds. At some later point, you may want to explore these possibilities. In *The 7 Secrets of Sound Healing,* I present a variation on this exercise that utilizes different pitches for the different vowel sounds.

For our purposes, in order to enhance our ability to vocalize the Divine Name, we're going to be sounding all the different vowels on the same pitch—using only one tone. This is called a *monotone*. This practice will be the most useful for learning to intone the Divine Name.

The harmonics in each of the vowel sounds will allow for different and specific resonances in your body and chakras. It's especially helpful if you place your intention, and your attention, on the particular chakra you're resonating.

The Vowel Sequence of the Alphabet

Frequently when the vowels are sounded, most people will automatically use a sequence they learned as children: *a-e-i-o-u*. This sequence has nothing to do with resonance or harmonics, or anything related to sound healing; this is simply the alphabetical order of the vowels—nothing more. It's not particularly effective if you're interested in learning about the qualities of resonance that the vowel sounds have and how this affects the physical body and the chakras.

The Vowel Sequence of the Chakras

The sequence of vowels and their resonant relationship to the chakras is this:

Vowel Sound	Chakra
UH (as in "huh")	1st—Root
OOO (as in "you")	2nd—Sacral
OH (as in "go")	3rd—Solar Plexus
AH (as in "ma")	4th—Heart
EYE (as in "my")	5th—Throat
AYE (as in "may")	6th—Third Eye
EEE (as in "me")	7th—Crown

On the facing page is an illustration of the vowel/chakra relationship that may assist you. It has proven very helpful as a visual aid when practicing this exercise. In addition, this vowel/chakra chart will be referred to throughout the various exercises in this book. Please feel free to copy the chart and use it alongside them.

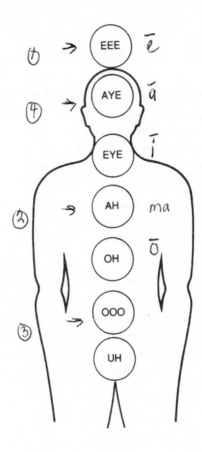

Track 2 on the Instructional CD will give you the pronunciation of the vowel sounds, allowing you the opportunity to hear how they sound when they're intoned as elongated vowel sounds. This will facilitate your sounding of the different exercises so that you may ultimately learn how to intone the Divine Name.

Remember, we all have different vocal ranges—especially men versus women. Women usually have a range that is an octave above that of men. We all have different pitches at which we're most comfortable making tones. For the first part of Track 2, I have sounded the vowel for the first chakra utilizing three different pitches so that you can find one that feels most comfortable for you and tone along with me. The intention isn't that you copy the exact note I create, but rather that you begin to find a pitch that is easiest and most comfortable for you. In other words, don't try to duplicate the pitches of my voice in these exercises. They're simply demonstrations of the sounds to assist you in creating your own. If the sound you're making feels strained, try going a little higher or lower until you feel comfortable and relaxed with the tone. Track 2 isn't the complete exercise that is presented in the following section, but rather, it provides examples of the sounds you'll use when you experience this exercise in its entirety.

Please listen to Track 2 on the Instructional CD.

This exercise will take approximately 20 minutes. Following completion of it, I advise being in a state of silence for ten minutes or more. Please allow for at least 30 minutes to fully experience the benefits of this powerful toning exercise.

Toning the Chakras

Step 1—First Chakra: Focus your attention on the first chakra, the root chakra, located at the base of the spine. The vowel sound for this chakra is "UH" (as in the word *huh*).

Begin to tone an "UH" sound. It should be soft and gentle, as should all the sounds you will be making during this exercise. Continue to focus your attention on the first chakra and project your intention so that you visualize the sound resonating at the base of your spine. Feel it vibrating here, and as it does, become aware that the energy center associated with this area is resonating, becoming balanced and aligned. Make this "UH" sound seven times.

Step 2—Second Chakra: Next, focus your attention on the second chakra, the sacral chakra, located about three inches below the navel. The vowel sound for this chakra is "OOO" (as in the word *you*).

Begin to tone a soft and gentle "OOO" sound. Continue to focus your attention on the second chakra and project your intention so that you visualize the sound vibrating this area. As you feel it resonate here, experience this energy center balancing and aligning with sacred sound. Make this "OOO" sound seven times.

Step 3—Third Chakra: Focus your attention on the third chakra, the solar-plexus chakra, located at the navel area and several inches above. The sound for this chakra is "OH" (as in the word *go*).

Begin to tone a soft and gentle "OH" sound. Continue to focus your attention on the third chakra and project your intention so that you visualize the sound vibrating this area. As you feel the vowel sound resonate here, experience this energy center being balanced and aligned through sacred sound. Make this "OH" sound seven times.

Step 4—Fourth Chakra: Focus your attention on the fourth chakra, the heart chakra, located in the center of the chest. The vowel sound for this chakra is "AH" (as in the word *ma*).

"AH" is often a sound we make when we're in love, and indeed, the heart chakra is the center associated with love. Begin to tone a soft and gentle "AH" sound. Continue to focus your attention on the fourth chakra and project your intention so that you visualize the sound vibrating this area. As you feel the vowel sound resonate here, experience this energy center becoming balanced and aligned through sacred sound. Make this "AH" sound seven times.

Step 5—Fifth Chakra: Focus your attention on the fifth chakra, the throat chakra. The vowel sound for this chakra is "EYE" (as in the word *my*).

Begin to tone a soft and gentle "EYE" sound. Continue to focus your attention on the fifth chakra and project your intention so that you visualize the sound vibrating this area. As you feel the vowel sound resonate here, experience this energy center becoming balanced and aligned through sacred sound. Make this "EYE" sound seven times.

Step 6—Sixth Chakra: Focus your attention on the sixth chakra, the third-eye chakra, located in the forehead between the eyes and slightly above them. The vowel sound for this chakra is "AYE" (as in the word *may*).

Begin to tone a soft and gentle "AYE" sound. Continue to focus your attention on the sixth chakra and project your intention so that you visualize the sound vibrating this area. As you feel the vowel sound resonate here, experience this energy center becoming balanced and aligned through sacred sound. Make this "AYE" sound seven times.

Step 7—Seventh Chakra: Focus your attention on the seventh chakra, the crown chakra, located at the top of the head. The vowel sound for this chakra is "EEE" (as in the word *me*).

Begin to tone a soft and gentle "EEE" sound. Continue to focus your attention on the seventh chakra and project your intention so that you visualize the sound vibrating this area. As you feel the vowel sound resonate here, experience this energy center becoming balanced and aligned through sacred sound. Make this "EEE" sound seven times.

Step 8—Silent Meditation: At the completion of this exercise, you may feel very light-headed. You've been sounding, resonating, and balancing your chakras as the energy moves up your spine into your head and above. Allow yourself a good 10 to 15 minutes for meditation, bringing your awareness fully back to everyday consciousness. At the close, be sure to ground yourself (which I'll explain how to do in the next section).

During workshops, I tell participants to take this opportunity to sit in silence and have the experience that will be of highest benefit at this point in their spiritual development. I suggest that this is a very nice place to be, so they should sit in a state of meditation and enjoy the experience.

To Ground Yourself

After you've completed the meditation, it's sometimes helpful to draw the energy slowly back down into your lower chakras and your body in order to ground yourself. To do this, begin to tone a midrange "AH" sound three times, bringing the energy first to the heart chakra. Then, after three slow breaths, tone three of the deepest "UH" sounds, bringing the energy back into the first chakra to completely ground yourself.

The Importance of Silence and Meditation

This entire exercise can take up to a half hour—sometimes an hour if you're having a particularly good meditation. It's extremely transformational, both during the toning, when you're resonating your chakras, and especially afterward while you're in silence. Many people have related that they've experienced their most profound inner journeys and meditations from this exercise. In workshops, participants are often in states of bliss during the meditation and frequently following it as well. This exercise truly allows you to experience an introduction to the transformational power of sound.

The Power and Safety of Sound

Sound can act like a psychoactive substance, altering and enhancing consciousness. The extraordinary thing about it is that not only is it entirely natural, but it's totally controllable and totally safe. The experiences that people have are benevolent, blissful, and beautiful. This is the wonder of self-created sacred sound—you're responsible for the creation of it, and wherever you go or whatever you do, it's completely natural and well within your control. If you need to stop the experience, all you have to do is open your eyes and take a few breaths and you're back. I can honestly report that out of the tens of thousands of people I've worked with using sacred sound, there have never been any adverse effects. During workshops, the only complaint I've received from people is that they've been brought back and been grounded too soon after the experience—they were having too much fun! I assure them that they can always return to wherever they were simply by continuing to practice this exercise.

Here are a few reminders when you do this exercise (especially the first time):

- Allow yourself enough time to really enjoy the benefits that accompany this toning practice.

- Only do this in a safe environment where you won't be disturbed, sitting in a comfortable chair or perhaps on the floor. (*Never* do this exercise in a car or standing up.)

- Allow yourself time after the meditation to relax and fully integrate the experience once you've grounded yourself. Don't come back from the meditation at the end, open your eyes, and immediately rush to pick up the kids at school or go into that business meeting. Honor this exercise, the power of sound, and the experience you've just had.

Practice and Integration

Once again, be sure to give yourself plenty of time. If you've had any difficulty feeling the resonance of the vowel sounds in your body and your chakras, know that the more you practice this exercise, the more you'll understand how powerful it is, and how to incorporate it into your life. The more you work with sound in this manner, the easier it will be to experience the power of your own self-created sounds. Like any other sort of exercise, it may take some time to become comfortable with it and to fully integrate it into your physical and subtle bodies. The more you do it, the more effective it will ultimately become.

In the next chapter, we'll continue with our step-by-step process of learning to vocalize the Divine Name—the Tetragrammaton—which will incorporate the use of the vowel sounds such as we have just worked with, as well as variants on this sequence. Each of the exercises is a progression in sonic wisdom, giving you knowledge and experience of the power of sacred sound.

Chapter Nine

Vowels as Mantra Sound Bites

*L*earning to sound the Divine Name is a step-by-step process of vibratory activation and initiation. The previous chapter, "Toning the Chakras," was essential in actualizing this important process. Even if someone were to be shown the different vowel sounds that are used in order to intone the Tetragrammaton, it's very doubtful that the person would be able to feel the power of the sound without first experiencing the exercises. What would come out would at best be a sequence of vowel sounds that was not only meaningless (as would be expected) but that would have little or no effect, since there wouldn't have been any prior relationship and experience with fully sounding the vowels.

The reason for this is that the sounds themselves, without the intention to properly resonate and feel them, are like eating a plastic meal, which may look like authentic food but in reality is tasteless and nonnutritious. In order to sound the Divine Name, you must actually experience the power of sound through the various exercises leading up to and including "Intoning the Divine Name." And of course, it's imperative to have a deep awareness of the Tetragrammaton, as the first part of this book has provided.

There are a number of additional exercises that are necessary to practice in order to fully experience and vocalize the sounding of the Divine Name. These exercises are based on "Toning the Chakras." I call them . . .

. . . Vowels as Mantra Sound Bites

In the last chapter, I focused upon toning the chakras as an extended exercise that is quite powerful. If you can feel and embody these sounds and utilize them on a daily basis, the effects can be dramatic and bring profound, positive changes into your life. When they're used as a daily practice, the results are phenomenal. Your entire being will change—from your nervous system to your chakra system. You'll become grounded yet more flexible. You'll be more creative and relaxed—more healthy and vibrant. And through the meditation that follows the exercise, your consciousness will be enhanced.

The next step to working with sound in order to learn to vocalize and intone the Divine Name is to introduce you to a shortened version of the sound exercise from the last chapter. As I've emphasized, doing this new one effectively requires that you have first had practice and experience with the extended exercise of "Toning the Chakras" from the previous chapter.

The different exercises that make up "Vowels as Mantra Sound Bites" are an abbreviated variation on the complete "Toning the Chakras." There is a progression involved in them and the particular sequence in which they're presented. It's necessary to learn them all in order to ultimately vocalize the Divine Name. To properly do so, you'll need to be able to sound all seven chakras with their corresponding vowel sounds on a single breath, starting at the crown center, going down to the root chakra, and then returning back up to the crown center. This can be quite challenging for most, and it's important to build up with easier exercises in order to gain this ability.

Through practicing these exercises and feeling the rapid resonance of the vowel sounds with your chakras, you'll be enhancing your ability to experience the sonic power of the Divine Name. "Vowels as Mantra Sound Bites" is presented as four separate exercises so that you'll have the experience of sounding the vowels in both ascending and descending order in a shorter amount of time.

Note: You may find it useful to consult the chakra/vowel–relationship chart on page 119 to assist you with these exercises. It's often helpful to close your eyes and place your hand in front of each chakra as you sound forth the vowel. And remember that the more you practice these exercises, the easier they will become, and the more you'll be able to actually experience their resonance and power.

Part I: One Breath for Each Vowel—Ascending Order

Please listen to Track 3 on the Instructional CD.

With this first exercise, you'll tone each chakra once with its designated vowel sound, using one breath. I invite you to take your time experiencing this, truly feeling the resonance of the sound in each specific chakra and its associated part of the body. You will be sounding each chakra with its vowel in ascending order, starting with the root and going up to your crown center.

These are the vowel sounds and their associated chakras that we will use for this first exercise:

Vowel Sound	Chakra
UH (as in "huh")	1st—Root
OOO (as in "you")	2nd—Sacral
OH (as in "go")	3rd—Solar Plexus
AH (as in "ma")	4th—Heart
EYE (as in "my")	5th—Throat
AYE (as in "may")	6th—Third Eye
EEE (as in "me")	7th—Crown

As with all the exercises in this book, find a place where you won't be disturbed. And of course, be sure that the pitch you use when you make your sound is easy, gentle, and comfortable for you—no straining or loud sounds allowed!

Follow these simple steps:

1. To begin, focus your attention on your root chakra and sound the "UH" while feeling this chakra being balanced and aligned.

2. Now, on your next breath, focus your attention on your sacral chakra and sound the "OOO" on this same note while feeling this chakra being balanced and aligned.

3. On your next breath, focus on the navel chakra, and on the same note, sound the "OH," feeling this chakra being balanced and aligned.

4. Now, focus on the heart with an "AH" on the same note, feeling this chakra being balanced and aligned.

5. Next, focus on your throat center with an "EYE" on the same note, feeling this chakra being balanced and aligned.

6. On the next breath, focus on your third eye with an "AYE" on the same note, feeling this chakra being balanced and aligned.

7. Finally, focus on your crown and sound forth an "EEE" on the same note, feeling this chakra being balanced and aligned with all of the others.

You've allocated one breath per vowel sound to resonate each chakra. This entire exercise can take approximately one minute. It's important and necessary for you to be able to actually feel the resonance of each chakra with the specific vowel when practicing it. If you're having difficulty with this, repeat these steps until you're comfortable using one breath for each chakra as you sound the associated vowel and until you're able to feel the resonance within your body, mind, and spirit.

Please take your time. And of course, be sure to allow enough time after the exercise to integrate and assimilate your experience.

Incidentally, you can practice this exercise several times, bringing the energy up your chakras as you focus on each one with a breath/vowel sound. The more you do so, the more you'll be astounded by the power of your own projected sound to resonate your chakras, regardless of the time you've spent making it.

Part II: One Breath for Each Vowel—Descending Order

Please listen to Track 4 on the Instructional CD.

Our next step in this process involves reversing the order of the vowel sequence, sounding each chakra going from the crown down to the root, using one breath per vowel sound. The combination of vowels in this sequence is:

Vowel Sound	Chakra
EEE (as in "me")	7th—Crown
AYE (as in "may")	6th—Third Eye
EYE (as in "my")	5th—Throat
AH (as in "ma")	4th—Heart
OH (as in "go")	3rd—Solar Plexus
OOO (as in "you")	2nd—Sacral
UH (as in "huh")	1st—Root

Start by focusing your intention on the crown chakra. Now sound the "EEE" of this chakra using one breath. On your next breath, do the same with the "AYE" vowel sound of the third-eye chakra. Continue in this manner all the way down to the root chakra, where you'll make the "UH" sound.

As always, be sure to allow enough time after the exercise to integrate and assimilate your experience.

Part III: One Breath for All Chakras—Ascending Order

Please listen to Track 5 on the Instructional CD.

Our next step in this process involves sounding the entire vowel sequence starting at the root chakra and going up to the crown chakra in one breath. This ability to sound all the chakras in one breath may prove quite challenging at first. Remember to take as deep a breath as you can and to be as relaxed as possible. This entire exercise may only take 15 or 20 seconds. With each of these "Vowels as Mantra Sound Bites" exercises, you'll be spending less and less time actually sounding each chakra. Nevertheless, it's extremely powerful. Focusing your intention on each chakra is helpful in order to experience and feel this.

As you sound all your chakras with one breath, you'll probably begin to hear the harmonics of the different vowel sounds. Some people find that if they slightly nasalize the sounds, the harmonics seem to become even more audible.

In addition, listening to the recorded example found on the Instructional CD will be very useful for you—it will provide a demonstration of the sounds, and a model of what these exercises can sound like. Remember, though, that we all have different voices—different vocal tones and different pitches that are unique to, and perfect for, each of us.

Also, please remember that with all these exercises, you're working with sacred sound. Don't forget to practice them in an appropriate place where you can be relaxed, feel attuned to the Divine, and won't be disturbed. And of course, never practice them in any situation where your attention to anything else is needed.

Take a deep breath and then sound the vowels in this order in one breath:

Vowel Sound	Chakra
UH (as in "huh")	1st—Root
OOO (as in "you")	2nd—Sacral
OH (as in "go")	3rd—Solar Plexus
AH (as in "ma")	4th—Heart
EYE (as in "my")	5th—Throat
AYE (as in "may")	6th—Third Eye
EEE (as in "me")	7th—Crown

Gaining the ability to sound all your chakras in one breath is crucial to learning to intone the Divine Name. Please continue to practice this exercise until you're comfortable resonating all your chakras in a single breath. Once you do gain this ability, you will truly be well on your way to becoming adept at working with sound.

Part IV: One Breath for All Chakras—Descending Order

Please listen to Track 6 on the Instructional CD.

After you've successfully completed sounding the chakras going from the root to the crown in one breath, the next step is to reverse this order. In one breath, you'll sound all the chakras from the seventh to the first, starting with the "EEE" sound at the crown center and working your way down, until you end on the root chakra with the "UH" sound.

The combination of vowels in this sequence is:

Vowel Sound	Chakra
EEE (as in "me")	7th—Crown
AYE (as in "may")	6th—Third Eye
EYE (as in "my")	5th—Throat

AH (as in "ma")	4th—Heart
OH (as in "go")	3rd—Solar Plexus
OOO (as in "you")	2nd—Sacral
UH (as in "huh")	1st—Root

The same principles from the last exercise apply to this one. This single-breath exercise takes approximately 20 seconds—sometimes an even shorter amount of time. Yet it's extremely important and powerful. It's also one of the basics for learning to intone the Divine Name. As with the last exercise, sounding the seven chakras in one breath can at first prove challenging. But as I mentioned before, the more you practice this, the more you'll be amazed by the power of your own projected sound to resonate your chakras.

Some Suggestions and Reminders

Before we continue with the next chapter, in preparation for intoning the Divine Name, I feel it is important to stress again how vitally sacred and significant this sound is. The reason this bears repeating is that this sound may simply be the *most* sacred and powerful on the planet. Thus, it's mandatory to remember two things:

1. Don't overdo it out of enthusiasm.
2. Honor the sacredness of this name.

It's quite possible that because of the power of this sound, you might become so enamored of the way it feels to intone it that you lose track of yourself. When you begin toning the complete set of vowel sounds, I ask that you have some sort of timer near you, and you not exceed sounding it for more than five minutes initially. After a few days, you can increase your time by another five minutes, and then again by another five minutes after a few more days. I'd like to suggest that you limit your total time sounding the Divine Name to a maximum of 15 minutes.

As you progress with these exercises, it's important to be aware of yourself, and if you feel any discomfort, please discontinue—even if you've found a pitch you really like that feels quite right for you. It's almost as though you're exercising a new muscle that needs care. Go slowly and gently with your toning. This isn't a contest of speed—to see how fast you can learn to make these sounds. Remember, sound is a great teacher. More important is the quality of that which you're experiencing—how it resonates as you feel it.

Know that while you've progressed to this level of sonic adeptness, you still have further to go. You haven't quite completed the training necessary to experience complete activation of the Divine Name.

Respect all of the sounds leading up to the intonation of the Tetragrammaton as being Divine—as if through them you're creating an etheric blessed object, placed on the altar of the temple that is your body. All of these sounds are holy. It's important to honor them.

As we move on to the next chapter, please remember that the same edict is echoed by one of the Ten Commandments: the Divine Name is sacred and must be treated as such.

Chapter Ten

The Technology of Intoning the Name

As mentioned throughout this book, my initial vocalization of the Divine Name was as a sequence of vowel sounds that utilized the harmonic series. It was an experience of energetic vibrational repatterning—a sound that brought the energy from above into my body and then back out again. As I made the sound, I felt the energy come into my crown center at the top of my head, travel down my chakras to my root chakra at the base of my spine, and then progress back out through the crown. This vocalization of the Divine Name initially was—and continues to be for me—an embodiment of light and love through sound.

I believe that as you proceed in your encounters with this sacred sound, the same will be true for you.

The key to this sonic practice is to first become comfortable intoning all seven of the sacred vowels in order to experience and feel their resonance in your chakras and corresponding parts of the body. As has been pointed out, this is usually not an ability that manifests immediately. It takes some practice, but like any sacred gift you receive, it's well worth it.

In the last chapter, we focused on gradually working up to experiencing the rapid resonance of the vowel sounds in the chakras with the various "Vowels as Mantra Sound Bites" exercises. We began at the root chakra, going through the intervening chakras on our way to the crown chakra. We then proceeded back from the crown down to the root chakra. We expanded our capacity to do so by going from taking one breath to resonate each chakra to taking one breath to resonate *all* the chakras.

Now, in our process of learning to sound the Divine Name, let's combine these methods, first going from crown to root, and then from the root back up to the crown.

Intoning the Divine Name

Note: As in the last chapter, you may find it useful to consult the chakra/vowel–relationship chart on page 119 to assist you with these exercises. Remember that it's often helpful to close your eyes and place your hand in front of each chakra as you sound forth the vowel. And keep in mind that the more you practice, the easier it will become, and the more you'll discover the power of your own self-created sound.

Part I: Two Breaths for All Chakras—
Descending and Ascending Order

Please listen to Track 7 on the Instructional CD.

For this next exercise, you'll be resonating all seven vowels in one breath, descending from the crown chakra to the root chakra. You'll take a brief pause, and then in the next breath, you'll continue by going from the root chakra, ascending back to the crown.

These are the vowel sounds and their associated chakras used for the first exercise:

Vowel Sound	Chakra
EEE (as in "me")	7th—Crown
AYE (as in "may")	6th—Third Eye
EYE (as in "my")	5th—Throat
AH (as in "ma")	4th—Heart
OH (as in "go")	3rd—Solar Plexus
OOO (as in "you")	2nd—Sacral
UH (as in "huh")	1st—Root

[Pause as you take another breath.]

UH (as in "huh")	1st—Root
OOO (as in "you")	2nd—Sacral
OH (as in "go")	3rd—Solar Plexus
AH (as in "ma")	4th—Heart
EYE (as in "my")	5th—Throat
AYE (as in "may")	6th—Third Eye
EEE (as in "me")	7th—Crown

This is an important step leading up to the actual intonation of the Divine Name. Essentially, you're just combining two of the exercises from the last chapter. Since you've already practiced and experienced those, doing this one shouldn't present major difficulties for you.

When you practice this exercise, feel the resonance of each chakra with its associated vowel sound, going down your chakras in one breath, and then going back up in another. Feel your different chakras being activated by each of the vowel sounds. This is necessary in order to truly experience the Divine Name.

As with the other exercises, you can do this one several times, bringing the energy down your chakras and then back up. Putting your hand in front of the chakra you're sounding helps focus your intention so that you can feel the energy from that chakra as it's being resonated. I trust that as you're experiencing this resonance, you're also hearing the descending and then ascending harmonics inherent in the vowel sounds. I like to think of this as climbing down and then up the sonic ladder.

After you've successfully practiced doing the preceding exercise in two breaths, one for going down the chakras and one for going up, you're ready for the next part.

Part II: One Breath for All Chakras— Descending and Ascending Order

Please listen to Track 8 on the Instructional CD.

Our final goal before actually intoning the Divine Name is for you to be able to complete this entire sequence in one breath. Now that you've been able to use two breaths to feel the resonance of each of the vowel sounds in your chakras, the next step is to intone all the vowels in *one* breath. This can prove challenging at first. The key is simply this: take a nice deep breath, be as relaxed as possible, and know that the duration of time you'll be able to sound each chakra will be very short. With the different exercises in this book, you've been slowly building your toning abilities, progressing toward this most important exercise. It may take some time to actually experience it, but you'll be able to successfully do it.

This is the order of the vowel sounds and their associated chakras that you'll use:

Vowel Sound	Chakra
EEE (as in "me")	7th—Crown
AYE (as in "may")	6th—Third Eye
EYE (as in "my")	5th—Throat
AH (as in "ma")	4th—Heart
OH (as in "go")	3rd—Solar Plexus
OOO (as in "you")	2nd—Sacral
UH (as in "huh")	1st—Root
OOO (as in "you")	2nd—Sacral
OH (as in "go")	3rd—Solar Plexus
AH (as in "ma")	4th—Heart
EYE (as in "my")	5th—Throat
AYE (as in "may")	6th—Third Eye
EEE (as in "me")	7th—Crown

When you sound all the chakras in descending and ascending order in one breath, there will be a shorter resonance of each vowel sound—probably about half the amount of time as in the previous exercises. It's important to be conscious of this. Be aware that in this exercise, it's only necessary to sound the root chakra ("UH") one time.

Remember that you've been building up to this. With each of the prior exercises, you've been experiencing the resonance of the vowel sounds with their associated chakras. You've done this going up and down, with one breath per chakra. You've also experienced this going up and down all your chakras, each time in one breath. You've continued practicing in the previous two exercises. Finally, now you've sounded all your chakras in both descending and ascending order in one breath.

As I've mentioned before, this ability to sound all your chakras on a single breath is necessary in order to intone the Divine Name. This was how I initially received the order of the vowels that provided my introduction to experiencing the Divine Name. It was how I learned to sound the Tetragrammaton. I pass this exercise on to you.

A Reminder

Once again, I'd like to remind you that listening to the Instructional CD will help you. In the recorded examples, I've utilized a normal breath—the type most people who aren't trained singers would take. I'm not using an "operatic" breath or creating an extended length of sound when I vocalize these exercises. My breath and the sounds I'm making are fairly standard, and normal for most people. As stated throughout this book, anyone can create this sound. I've taught this technique to total neophytes in the arena of making self-created sound, and they were able to do it. With a little practice, you'll be able to as well. Once you become "attuned" to this exercise, you're ready for the final step of creating the Divine Name.

When you sounded the vowels for all the chakras in descending and ascending order on one breath, it's quite likely that you heard something else besides just the vowels—something that sounded very much like an extended intonation of "Yahweh." Indeed, this *is* what you were hearing—the Divine Name.

The Four Vowels of the Divine Name

Remember, in Hebrew the Divine Name is written as יהוה. In English, this has been translated into the letters *YHVH* (Yod, Hey, Vav, Hey) and is often pronounced "Yahweh." In Chapter 3, we discussed in detail how the authentic sounding of the Hebrew letters of the Tetragrammaton—the Divine Name—is actually a sequence of vowel sounds: EEE—AH—OOO—AYE.

For the last exercise in this chapter, I'd like you to sound these four vowel sounds in a fluid, continuous manner. As you're doing so, feel the energy go from the top of your head, through your body to your root chakra, and then ultimately back up to the crown. As previously noted, one of the great tools to facilitate this is *visualization*—focusing your intention on what you're doing while making the sound.

Gliding Vowels

As you go through these vowel sounds, EEE—AH—OOO—AYE, it will take approximately three to four seconds to sound each one. Instead of the combined sequence of all the descending and ascending vowels used in the last exercise, you will only sound four. Yet you'll be able to feel *all* the vowels resonating your chakras. This is because of gliding vowel sounds, called *diphthongs,* which occur when two vowels are blended and connected in a continuous progression.

These gliding vowel sounds actually constitute one of the principal techniques for learning to create vocal harmonics. As you go in this specific order, EEE—AH—OOO—AYE, you'll be aware that there are other sounds occurring. You'll hear additional vowels or harmonics and feel their resonance.

By going from the "EEE" to the "AH" in a continuous, slow flow without stopping, you'll notice that you're actually passing through several vowel sounds (and their associated harmonics). You'll not only experience the "EEE" of the crown chakra and the "AH" of the heart chakra, but you'll also briefly hear and feel the resonance of both the third-eye and throat chakras.

This phenomenon is experienced even more in the next two vowels. In that same continuous breath, when you change from the "AH" to the "OOO" sound, you'll find other chakras being resonated that weren't deliberately sounded. Finally, on the last vowel, going from the "OOO" to the "AYE," you'll notice a whole series of vowels as you feel the resonance of the energy going up from your trunk to your head.

In truth, you'll be able to cover the entire gamut of vowel sounds from the previous exercises using only these four. This was an occurrence I first noticed while intoning what are considered to be the vowel letters of ancient Hebrew, יהוה, "EEE—AH—OOO— AYE," which make up the Divine Name. When I tried intoning this combination of vowels in a slow and continuous manner, I realized that I was creating virtually the same sound as when I'd vocalized the entire vowel spectrum.

When you listen to Track 9 and compare it to Track 8, you'll hear this. The major difference for me in using the four vowel sounds of the Tetragrammaton was that it was both easier and even more powerful. As you listen, be aware of the flexibility and fluidity of my enunciation of the vowel sounds while I demonstrate this.

In the other exercises, we specifically intoned each vowel separately. With this one, a key is to blend the vowel sounds together.

Part III: Sounding the Divine Name

Please listen to Track 9 on the Instructional CD.

(Please note that with this recorded example, as with the very first one in Track 2, I'm intoning the Divine Name in three different pitches: low, midrange, and high. For this particular sound, I often like to intone the Divine Name in a slightly higher pitch than normal—it allows me to hear the harmonics of this extraordinary sound more prominently and feel the resonance of the vowels more powerfully.)

As you sound the Divine Name using these four vowels, EEE—AH—OOO—AYE, let yourself be flexible and fluid in your enunciation. Blending them allows these gliding multiple-vowel sounds to emerge. Listening to Track 9 on the CD will make this sonic revelation self-evident. As I mentioned in the last section, if you compare it to the previous track, it's almost identical, yet I'm only sounding these four vowels.

In addition, as with the exercises in the preceding sections and chapters, you may find it useful to consult the chakra/vowel–relationship chart on page 119 to assist you.

1. To begin, make the sound "EEE," feeling the energy resonating your crown center.

2. Slowly change this "EEE" to the "AH" sound, and feel the energy move down through your third-eye and throat chakras into your heart chakra. As you go from "EEE" to "AH," you'll hear the sound "Yah" being created.

3. Slowly change this "AH" sound to that of "OOO." Feel the energy move down through your solar-plexus and sacral chakras. When you create this "OOO" sound, be fluid and flexible. Gently glide this "OOO" and gradually allow it to turn into an "UH" sound—that is, "OOO-UH." It will be subtle, but you'll feel this gliding vowel resonate your root chakra.

4. Slowly transition from this last sound to an "AYE"
    sound. Gently glide this "AYE" (as in "may") and
    slowly allow it to turn into an "EEE" (as in "me")—
    "AY-EEE." As it does so, you'll find you can feel
    this resonate in your crown center.

At the completion of this exercise, you'll have resonated
all your chakras. In addition, you should have heard the sound
"Yahweh." Creating other vowels through vocalizing the four
specific vowels of EEE—AH—OOO—AYE is one of the most
important keys to sounding the Divine Name. Once again, with
this particular exercise, listening to the recorded example on
Track 9 will be invaluable.

Practicing the Exercise

When properly intoned, יהוה (EEE—AH—OOO—AYE), the
Divine Name as vowels, will take the same amount of time as in
the previous exercise when you sounded all of the vowel sounds
in descending and then ascending order on one breath—about
15 seconds. By this point in your sonic development, you'll
have achieved the ability to feel all the different vowel sounds
resonating your chakras. It takes a bit of practice, but it truly is
worth it. For many, sounding these four vowels is actually less

difficult than doing so for the entire sequence of vowel sounds in our previous exercises.

Is it easy? No—it does take practice. Is it possible to do? Yes—many have learned to sound the Divine Name with just a little effort and persistence. Is it worth it? Experience it for yourself! I trust you'll find that it more than meets your expectations.

Through sounding EEE—AH—OOO—AYE in this manner, you'll be able to feel the resonance of the vowels and their harmonics as they change from one to another, vibrating your chakras . . . coming from the top of your head to the base of your trunk, and then back again. This is the sound of spirit coming into matter and then going back into spirit. It is the feeling of Divine Light and Sound entering the body and then ultimately leaving once more.

Through this process, we achieve a connection with Source, feeling truly attuned, in an almost psychotropic state in which we're in communion with the Divine. It is amazing and phenomenal and so sacred.

As you honor the sacredness of the Divine Name, please remember to allow plenty of time to return to a normal state of consciousness after you've experimented with this exercise. (And of course, as always, do this exercise in a place where you won't be disturbed.) You'll find it's extremely powerful, and you'll want to give adequate time to experiencing and appreciating this extraordinary sound.

Now that you've successfully learned to sound the Divine Name, in the next chapter, we'll add the final ingredient—prayer. Without incorporating this practice into the sounding of the Divine Name, it's not complete. Although there's still great power in this sound (you'll certainly be able to feel its resonance and energy), it's not nearly as great and all-encompassing as it is when coupled with the consciousness of prayer. Remember the formula *Frequency + Intent = Healing.* It takes both components—the sound as well as the energy that is encoded upon it—to create the overall extraordinary manifesting power of the Divine Name.

Please listen to Track 10 on the Instructional CD.

Chapter Eleven

The Divine Name as Prayer

*Y*ou've now reached the place in this book where all the information and exercises come together. Indeed, my goal in writing *The Divine Name* has been to empower you with the ability to use this extraordinary sound for prayer. As has been pointed out, this book is a step-by-step process of vibratory activation using sacred sound. You're now at the stage where you can begin to achieve a new level of being by using the Divine Name as prayer.

If, as we suppose, the Divine Name truly is the universal sound of God—a lost sound that we have rediscovered—it seems that the most appropriate and natural use of this name would indeed be as the ultimate form of prayer.

Prayer: An "Attitude of Gratitude"

Prayer means many things to many people. *Merriam-Webster's Collegiate Dictionary* defines it as "an address (as a petition) to God or a god in word or thought." Usually, this involves some sort of "asking" for something—most frequently prayers involve requests for healing or the granting of wishes. As previously noted, however, the most effective form of prayer is as an act of thankfulness energetically offered from the heart, as though that which is being asked for has already happened.

The true power of prayer occurs when our thoughts and emotions combine to create a heart-centered feeling. This power focuses on gratitude, as if the outcome we desire has already manifested. As I touched upon in Chapter 4, for the most effective prayer and manifestation to occur, you must "give thanks" for what you're praying for. This "attitude of gratitude," the heart-centered feeling of appreciation, is perhaps the single most important aspect of prayer.

Particularly with regard to using the Divine Name, we should be clear about our prayers and ensure that they are for the highest good of all—ourselves, others, and the planet. I'd like to suggest that we try to embody the words of St. Francis: "Lord, make me an instrument of Your peace." This seems a perfect petition to God. If we can be focused on compassion and kindness, rather than competition, then it feels like our prayers are in alignment with the true purpose of using the Divine Name.

Sarah Benson, one of my greatest teachers in the field of sound healing, always stressed the importance of being a conduit of the sacred sound—of moving out of its way so that the Divine and Sacred could take over and come through it. I pass her wisdom on to you.

The Power of the Heart

Prayer, as we've approached it, is a "heart-based" phenomenon. A key to utilizing it in this manner—especially with the Divine Name—is to truly understand the power of our hearts. How *does* the heart fit into this?

Different spiritual teachers and groups have known about the extraordinary power of the heart for millennia. Now, its power is being validated by modern science—not just as an organ that pumps blood through the body, but as far more. Most modern-day readers are aware that the brain—what is perceived to be our organ of thought—produces electrical and magnetic impulses, waves that have been studied in medicine for many years.

What has only recently been discovered and is less well known is that the heart generates the body's most powerful and extensive electromagnetic field. Compared to the brain, the electrical component of the heart's field may be up to 60 times greater in amplitude. This energy permeates every cell in the body. The heart's magnetic component has the potential of being approximately 5,000 times stronger than the brain's, and can be detected several feet away from the body with sensitive magnetometers.

From one perspective, it seems as if the heart, our organ of feeling, is more powerful than the brain, our organ of thinking. It is almost as though the brain is a trigger mechanism for focusing the greater electromagnetic energy of the heart.

Coherent Waves

The experience of positive emotions, such as love or appreciation, creates a coherent pattern in the heart's rhythmic activity that is smooth and ordered. When this happens, these emotions change the heart's beating patterns, corresponding with changes in the structure of the electromagnetic field that is radiated. In contrast, negative emotions, such as anger or frustration, are associated with an incoherent wave pattern that is erratic and disordered.

Much of this research into the power of the heart comes from the Institute of HeartMath. Investigators have shown that the capacity of the heart to create enormous electromagnetic fields arises when it is in a state of *coherence.* This occurs when the waves being generated by the heart are in resonance with other bodily systems, such as respiration and brain waves. The heart and all these other systems operate at the same frequency, vibrating together in rhythmic harmony, which allows the tremendous electromagnetic field to manifest.

When we're in a happy and loving state, generating positive emotions such as love or appreciation, the heart is in a state of coherence. When this occurs, we're creating an extremely strong electromagnetic field, with extraordinary potential for manifesting the power of prayer.

However, when we experience negative feelings such as anger, anxiety, fear, or frustration, the rhythms between our heart, brain, and other bodily systems are out of harmony. During such times, the electromagnetic waves that manifest are scattered and disorganized. These are *incoherent waves.* The electromagnetic field generated is extremely diminished. Such chaotic frequencies aren't positive for either our health or our prayers.

The Fail-Safe Mechanism of Prayer

Since the power of prayer is a heart-based phenomenon, we create a weakened field from our heart when we produce incoherent waves. Our prayers at such times aren't effective. This is one of the "fail-safe" mechanisms of prayer, and especially the use of Divine Name—it can't be effective when we're not in a positive place. At best, the improper prayer is totally ineffectual. At worst, it could cause an imbalance in anyone misusing it.

According to many spiritual sources, attempting to project negative energy through prayer simply backfires. It not only doesn't work, but whatever is negatively sent out seems to come back to adversely affect the person who transmitted it. This perhaps is a demonstration of the effect described at the end of the Third Commandment, which warns that those who attempt to misuse the Divine Name receive retribution. Thus, using prayer while generating an incoherent wave just doesn't work.

Creating Coherent Waves

It's possible to learn to generate a coherent field of the heart through different meditation practices that utilize specific visualization techniques. The coherent wave of the heart has the ability to directly interact with our emotions, and when this wave manifests, we frequently find ourselves in a happy and loving state. In fact, when we effectively practice this technique, we're able to change any disharmonious and negative feelings into harmonious and positive ones.

There is a particular method I'd like to share with you that amplifies the ability to manifest a heartfelt condition for prayer. It generates an extraordinary source of positive energy, which can be focused, and it produces even greater amounts of positive energy through use of the Divine Name. Much of this process is based upon material that comes from the Institute of HeartMath, as well as the work of Gregg Braden, among others. I've modified this process in order to create the following technique. From my experience, the method I'm about to share is easy to implement and extremely effective:

> *To begin, simply take a few nice deep breaths. Breathe deeply and slowly, feeling the air fill your lungs. The slower and deeper the breath, the better. When you inhale, feel your breath coming in—not only through your nose or mouth, but also through your very heart. This is a crucial element in this breathing technique. As you exhale, visualize your breath expanding out—not only through your nose or mouth, but also from your heart region.*

While you are in this state of breathing slowly, visualize your breath coming in and going out through your heart center. You're now beginning to create a coherent field between your heart and brain.

Next, as you continue breathing in this manner, simply begin feeling appreciation for something—it could be a partner or spouse, a child, a pet, a beautiful sunset, the sound of waves lapping against a beach, or perhaps a mountain spring—it doesn't matter what. All that matters is that you feel a sense of appreciation.

Feeling appreciation is extremely effective, especially for generating the power of prayer. This may be *the* most important aspect of empowering prayer.

Throughout this entire book, I've shared that sound, particularly sacred sound, is composed not only of the sound itself, but also of the intent and prayer encoded upon it. Thus, for the full utilization of the Divine Name, we must use it for its ultimate purpose—as prayer.

The Divine Name as Sonic Offering

One final suggestion I'd like to make before we begin intoning the Divine Name as prayer is to conceive of it as a sonic offering to the Creator. In many different traditions, offerings such as the lighting of incense or candles are made before the actual prayer. With this in mind, we can intone the Divine Name as a sonic version of this, projecting this offering onto our prayers. Not only are we praying in a manner of appreciation, giving thanks for all that is—we are concurrently generating offerings to the Divine. This is another form of manifesting gratitude for all that is. Think of your sound as a way of giving thanks to the Creator for the blessings you're co-creating.

In the previous chapter and all the others in Part III leading up to it, we worked with the vowel sounds to resonate our chakras. We ultimately learned to sound the Tetragrammaton, toning יהוה as four different vowel sounds: EEE—AH—OOO—AYE.

It's now time to learn the technique for utilizing the Divine Name as prayer. The following steps allow us to pray on a personal level and then expand our prayers until they ultimately incorporate a universal level of consciousness.

Utilizing the Divine Name as Prayer

Part I

— Find yourself a comfortable space where you won't be disturbed. It's best if this is a contemplative or sacred place where you can meditate/pray and make sound.

— Sit comfortably, with your spine straight and your eyes closed.

— Next, add the visualization of breathing in and breathing out through your heart area.

— Now, begin to feel gratitude and appreciation for someone or something. This will place you in a state of receptivity that will allow you to communicate with Source. Be in a state of appreciation—maintaining an "attitude of gratitude" for all that is.

Part II

**It may be helpful to again listen to Track 9
on the Instructional CD.**

— Vocalize the vowel sounds you've learned that compose the Divine Name, toning "EEE—AH—OOO—AYE" one time. Feel the energy of these sounds as they resonate from the top of your head down into your body, and then back again out your head, creating a connection between you and the Divine. Send this energy out from yourself to the Higher Power as you make this sound. Become aware of the positive feelings being generated and the feeling of love that radiates through and from you.

Part III

— Next, begin to audibly give thanks for that which you have, or offer your appreciation for what you would *like* to have in your life as though it is already a fact. Some examples of this might be:

- *Thank you for my partner (my children, my . . .).*
- *Thank you for my health.*
- *Thank you for my prosperity.*

— Each time you give thanks for something, vocalize the Divine Name, "EEE—AH—OOO—AYE," one time, feeling the energy resonate through you and sending the sound out to the Divine.

Part IV

— Continue to speak aloud, giving thanks for that which you would like to co-create on a more expansive level as though it has already occurred.
Some examples of this might be:

- *Thank you for the support of my business.*
- *Thank you for the harmony in my marriage.*
- *Thank you for the peace in my life.*

— Each time you give thanks for something, vocalize the Divine Name, "EEE—AH—OOO—AYE," one time, feeling the energy resonate through you and sending this sound out to the Divine.

Part V

— Conclude by stating aloud that which you would like to co-create on a universal level as though it has already occurred. Some examples of this might be:

- *Thank you for peace on the planet.*
- *Thank you for the harmony of the environment.*
- *Thank you for the love and kindness that all humans share.*

— Each time you give thanks for something, vocalize the Divine Name, "EEE—AH—OOO—AYE," one time, feeling the energy resonate through you and sending this sound out to the Divine.

Part VI

— After completing your prayers, sit in a state of silence, receptivity, and gratitude for the experience you've just had. Be open to receiving information, thoughts, ideas, and feelings from the Divine. Allow yourself sufficient time to fully experience this exercise. You may find yourself in quite a transcendent state as a result of using the Divine Name in this manner.

This, of course, is just one manner in which to pray. As you might have noticed, with these particular steps, we go from utilizing prayer on an individual level to a universal one. However, please do as you are inwardly guided. You might want to focus first on giving thanks for global situations such as peace, and then focus on personal prayers. The manner of prayer presented here is simply one model that might be helpful. There are numerous ways of giving prayerful thanks, but they *all* involve a modality utilizing breath, feeling, and sound. From my perspective, the use of the Divine Name as a sacred technology to enhance these prayers is a joyous technique I am honored to share.

The Divine Name as Healing

My wife, Andi, who is my co-author of *Tantra of Sound: Frequencies of Healing,* has suggested:

> The Divine Name, when utilized in this manner of prayer, offers us a direct connection to the Divine and awakens the Divine in ourselves. When we are in a state of resonance with

the Divine, we are in a state of perfection. As this occurs, we achieve frequency shifts that put us into balance and harmony. Therein lies the healing.

I concur.

While our focus in this chapter has been on the use of the Divine Name for prayer, I'd like to mention that there have been many reports of deep healings spontaneously being experienced under these circumstances. These seemingly miraculous occurrences may be a gift from the Creator as a result of having properly used the Divine Name.

In conclusion, after you've done the preceding exercise and you're in a state of deep meditation, if you feel that you need further clarification on what's appropriate to personally pray for, just check in with yourself and let your inner guidance give you direction.

Now let's move on to how we might use the Divine Name to really make some big changes!

Part IV

Finale

Chapter Twelve

The Sound That Can Change the World

In music, the *Finale* is defined as the closing part of a composition. For many, it is also considered the grand ending, and offers the greatest composite of sounds from the piece. In this last chapter, I trust I'll be offering you the true culmination of all the information, recordings, and exercises in this book—what I consider to be the most important purpose of the Divine Name: its use as an extraordinary means of accelerating our collective evolution, with the ability to create a quantum leap in our consciousness.

In the previous chapter, we focused on the use of the Divine Name for personal prayer. Such a use can, of course, embrace the concept of planetary peace and healing, but it was introduced as an individually oriented modality. What if this sound *could* be used to create oneness and unify the planet? What if the Divine Name might somehow be utilized as a universal sound, created en masse for this purpose?

We've reached the point in this book where you can sound the Divine Name and utilize it effectively in your prayers. It is now time to explore its use as the sound that can change the world.

The Universal Sound

The Divine Name is universal. So often people from different religious paths won't engage in the sacred chanting of another tradition because the words seem foreign to them. But because the Divine Name as presented in this book is composed entirely of vowels, no one can object to working with it. Vowels are trans-denominational—found within all traditions, cultures, and sacred sounds.

Anyone who has practiced the exercises in the manner taught herein can experience the vowels in a similar fashion. You will feel the energy come in through the crown chakra, pass through the other chakras to the root, and then return up through the crown—a sonic example of spirit going into matter and then going back into spirit. This is not theory. Once you've learned to sound the Divine Name and feel its resonance, this then becomes *experience.* Once this has happened, it is real—at least for *you.* And anyone else who has experienced this will also know it. Thus, these exercises provide universal effects.

Because of the trans-denominational nature of vowel sounds, as well as their universal effect, it is my great hope that the Divine Name will be recognized and embraced as a global sound of unity and peace, and that through this recognition, we may all sound this name together.

Global Harmonization

Often when I'm in deep meditation, I find myself in contact with a source of wisdom that offers me great guidance. Thirty years ago during such a meditation, I was given an "assignment" to help bring awareness of the use of sound and music for healing to this planet. I worked fervently in order to accomplish that. More than ten years ago, I was again in contact with this same numinous energy. I asked if I'd fulfilled this assignment. Was my purpose complete? It seemed that after several books, numerous CDs, and years of teaching, there certainly was a great deal of awareness of the power of sound for healing, and that this consciousness was continuing to grow.

The reply I was given was short and simple . . . and deeply profound—at least for me. I was told that along with using sound for personal healing, I was to begin to apply it toward *planetary* healing. This continues to be a part of my purpose and is the focus of this chapter.

For the last decade, since that deep inner encounter, I've been utilizing the term I came up with (which I mentioned in Chapter 1) that encompasses this concept: *Global Harmonization*—facilitating the manifestation of peace and harmony on this planet. For me, the use of intentionalized sacred sound to accomplish this is most powerful and natural. As noted previously, there is a term from Kabbalah that mirrors this. *Tikkun Olam* is a phrase that can mean mending or repairing the world. From my perspective, the greatest aspect of Global Harmonization would be to achieve Tikkun Olam through the use of the Divine Name.

The Golden Rule

In all the different spiritual traditions, there exists some form of what we call the Golden Rule. This idea is most frequently understood as "Do unto others as you would have them do unto you."

We can ultimately acknowledge this as simply meaning "Be kind to each other." This understanding of treating each other as we would treat ourselves is a common thread—a universal concept of spiritual and mystical teachings throughout the world. *Love yourself and love others equally.* Many conceive of the Golden Rule as the global ethic that, when practiced, enables us to embody compassion. Whenever we pray with the energy of the Golden Rule, we are indeed in resonance with the Divine. In addition, when we're in resonance with *each other* in this way, all barriers that exist between us disappear. We realize that we are one, and as we experience this, we manifest the compassion necessary for the enhanced activation of our consciousness—we evolve to another level of being. Quite simply, by embodying the Golden Rule, we can manifest Tikkun Olam.

It is the potential of healing the world through sound that is my greatest hope for the outcome of this book. This chapter provides the intended result of all the other material and practices we've worked with—using the Divine Name to heal the planet. Through sharing proper understanding and knowledge of what the Divine Name is and how to vocalize it, we make a technology that can change the world available to all people.

In previous chapters, we've built up to using the Divine Name as a means for our individual connection with the Divine. Using it in this way in our meditations and prayers can create extraordinary change for ourselves. But there is another level at which to do so: to utilize its power through group consciousness in order to create planetary transformation, initiating global harmony, peace, and healing. When it's sounded on a global level, we can create resonance with others throughout the world, raising our consciousness and enhancing our evolution. Thus, we can unify the planet and allow the interconnection between us to emerge and manifest.

I'll share with you how this can be accomplished.

A Time of Great Changes

To begin, let's first acknowledge that we're indeed living in tumultuous times. Whether it's famine, disease, genocide, pollution, climate change, war, the economy, or whatever else you want to focus on, we're facing numerous extremely difficult challenges. There are enormous global issues at stake as we progress in the 21st century.

Prophecies and predictions about this period are found in diverse traditions. Many perceive this to be a time of remarkable change and transition. Others think of it in a less-than-positive light. Some call it the "Great Shift," while others refer to it as the "End Times." Particular focus has been given to the year 2012 as a culminating point for these shifts. Regardless of what precise name or exact date you give it, this juncture in time and space seems to be very special and crucial. It merits our immediate attention.

An Evolutionary Shift of Consciousness

Most of the issues that are facing us seem to have been created by humans. Most can also be *resolved* through human activity. What is necessary is that we as a species overcome our petty differences and incessant competition and begin to cooperate, manifesting compassion. This requires nothing less than creating an evolutionary leap in our consciousness.

Through our consciousness, we can co-create a "consensus" reality, based on mutually agreed-upon thoughts, feelings, and beliefs. Many of our greatest scientists are now in alignment with ancient spiritual masters who have told us that this is possible. Our faith can indeed move mountains—particularly when utilized in conjunction with a technology as powerful as sounding the Divine Name.

One person, even one country, may not have the power or the ability to make the changes necessary to repair all the damage that has been done through negligence, denial, and pure foolishness. The focus of consciousness and activity needed to fix these issues demands cohesive global unity. This planet must work together as one.

The human race as a species needs to evolve to a level of consciousness where we understand that we can no longer successfully exist as solitary units that remain isolated from one another. As individual villages, tribes, cities, or states, we can't do separately what needs to be done to repair the damage that's been created. We must learn to work together as a compassionate and caring species, assisting each other, and as we do so, assisting the planet itself. From one perspective, the solution to how to create the changes necessary to save the planet is simple: we must unify our consciousness. The question, of course, is . . . *how can this be accomplished?*

Using the Divine Name

One answer is this: by working together with intentionalized sound—vocalized prayer—and in particular, by utilizing the extraordinary power and consciousness inherent in the Divine Name. It seems that what was once seemingly impossible and miraculous is now both possible and real, and can be achieved through the remarkable technology that incorporates the personal name of God.

This concept—that we may somehow collectively be able to interface with each other and affect the consciousness of this planet—may for some seem unimaginable. But it is *real*. For millennia, our mystical and wise ancestors have told us of the power of prayer and of the ability to create change on both a personal and planetary level through collective consciousness. We've been told that we can usher in a new era—a new world of peace and harmony.

Now scientists who are exploring this area are echoing these thoughts. The results of new research reveal that we can individually interface with "reality" and affect it. And when we work together, this effect can be greater than ever imagined.

At the present time, individually we may have only limited access to our ability to influence the universe. But when we gather together, this co-creation can become extraordinary. During collective peace meditations, for example, in which participating individuals actually "felt" the energy of peace within themselves while they meditated, it was found that violent and aggressive behavior dropped considerably within the cities where these meditations occurred—usually for nearly 24 hours after such activities. Later, more advanced global peace prayers demonstrated even more remarkable results.

Global Consciousness Project

I'd like to bring your attention to the Global Consciousness Project (GCP), originally initiated at Princeton University. This project is composed of scientists, engineers, researchers, and many others who have been exploring a rather curious phenomenon: the "consciousness" of the planet. The GCP seems to have come upon a technology that is able to actually measure this. They have more than 40 devices, called random number generators (nicknamed EGGs or eggs), which are spread throughout the world. As the name would suggest, these EGGs generate random numbers. But after global events of high compassion, researchers noticed something strange. When they analyzed the data afterward, the numbers from these EGGs became *less* random. The results were impressive: instead of the straight line that should occur randomly, a wave emerged, which seems to indicate that events of global significance are measurable and may be representative of the consciousness of the planet. It's almost as though consciousness itself can be charted through these EGGs.

What is both interesting and important about the effects of positive events such as global meditations and prayers is that the number of people it takes to create a noticeable change in the consciousness of the planet is quite small. There is a critical mass necessary to manifest change, and the number is, in fact, extraordinarily trifling: the square root of one percent of the population. With a planet of six billion, this amounts to around 8,000 people. Think about that! In order to make a change in the consciousness of the planet, it's only necessary that a tiny number of people engage in an activity such as a global meditation or peace prayer.

Global Coherence Initiative

Along with the work of the Global Consciousness Project to measure shifts and changes in the planet, there is the Global Coherence Initiative, a HeartMath-launched global monitoring system that uses a series of newly designed sensors deployed across the earth in order to specifically measure the changes in the geomagnetic field.

The concept of this monitoring is simple—as noted in previous chapters, there is an electromagnetic field created by the individual human heart. This field is spectacularly large if the heart is in coherence. Our planet also has a magnetic field, the *ionosphere,* which is measurable by satellites orbiting the earth. Many scientists believe that this geomagnetic field is able to affect our emotions and our consciousness. The Global Coherence Initiative is trying to determine if there is a relationship between the individual fields generated by our hearts and the geomagnetic field. All indications thus far are that there is indeed such a relationship—a feedback loop in which our personal fields and the planetary field interface and can influence each other. In particular, this effect seems to be most powerful when we as a species are generating a unified field through coherence of our hearts.

It appears that the geomagnetic field is able to affect the emotions of individuals on this planet, and that the fields produced by people—particularly those resonating in coherence together—are able to likewise affect the planet's field. We humans, as a conscious group creating coherence of the heart, can collectively influence the geomagnetic field. This is remarkable. It demonstrates a unification principle—that we as a species can resonate collectively to be as one, not only with each other, but with all things, including the earth.

While the Global Consciousness Project and the Global Coherence Initiative are measuring different phenomena, they both acknowledge the exceptional power of our collective consciousness. These organizations have now united in order to provide further validation that we as a species can affect different types of energetic fields on the earth. In this way, we can assist the planet, perhaps enhancing planetary consciousness and evolution, creating a kinder world and a better tomorrow.

World Sound Healing Day

The power of sound to amplify prayer has been discussed again and again in this book. There are now several global sound-healing events—most significantly, World Sound Healing Day, which I initiated in 2000, taking place each February 14: Valentine's Day. On this day, thousands of people all over the world tone the "Ah" sound, encoded with the intention of peace and harmony, sending a sonic valentine of love throughout the planet. These planetary toning events also occur at other times during the year, and they do make a difference.

On the next page is a chart, courtesy of the Global Consciousness Project, of World Sound Healing Day on February 14, 2009. While there are many variables inherent in analyzing the data, GCP director Roger Nelson stated: "This looks like a confirmation of the idea that large scale communal thought and emotion may show up as structure in our data." In addition, he observed, "The outcome is a remarkably strong deviation" from the traditional straight line that normally appears, and he found the results "quite encouraging" with regard to demonstrating the power of intentionalized sound.

This chart is of a 24-hour period for February 14, 2009. The term *UTC* in the chart is short for "Coordinated Universal Time," a very accurate time scale that couples Greenwich mean time with atomic time. The "Eggs" referenced are the random number generators previously described in this chapter. The graph reflects data from 61 of these. You'll notice a strong rise in the graph, particularly around the time of both a global meditation that occurred on that day (marked "medit") and after the global "Ah" tone ("toning"). I've found it of interest that sometimes the GCP charts indicate changes in the data *after* the event—as though it takes a while for the energy to register.

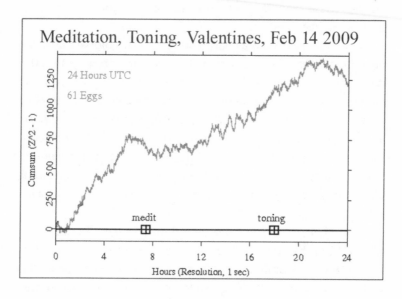

Meditation, Toning, Valentines, Feb 14 2009

Now that you have experienced the power of sound to shift and change energy on a personal level through the Divine Name, it's time to become aware of the power of sound to change the consciousness of the planet itself. If possible, join with others during any of the many global peace events that take place. If people don't already know about the power of sound to amplify their consciousness and thoughts (and they may not), share with them what *you* know. Remember that in Dr. Emoto's water experiments, polluted and mudlike water became clear and crystalline after it had been vocally prayed over. Our vocalized prayers have the ability to change not only molecular structure, but both personal and planetary consciousness as well.

Sound is a multidimensional energy, and it adheres to modern quantum physics, which suggests that time and space don't really create the limitations that we once believed. Experiments have shown that electrons separated by significant distances can simultaneously be affected by consciousness. So can our DNA. Our feelings, intentions, and prayers seem to be major ingredients of this effect. As I've continually pointed out, sound is able to amplify these ingredients, and thus enhance our ability to effect change in the very creation of reality.

Miracle as Technology

From all indications, sound coupled with intent is able to influence our planetary field and our consciousness. To many, this would be a miracle, but as my colleague Gregg Braden has noted, when the actual mechanism of a miracle is understood, it then becomes a technology. Thus, the knowledge of how to utilize sound to change our consciousness can be considered a form of technology.

I would further speculate that if an understanding of the power of prayer and sound is a technology, then knowledge of the proper sounding of the Divine Name, as you've learned through this book and the Instructional CD, is a gigantic step forward in this technology—perhaps like going from a Model T to a spaceship, although no analogy seems quite appropriate, especially since we're dealing with a technology of the heart, not the mind.

As noted, a difference between technology and technique is that the former is the knowledge, while the latter is the application and use of this knowledge. Thus, our ability to sound the Divine Name is a technique that can enhance our prayers, put us in contact with the Divine, manifest change, and indeed create miracles. It is one that has the potential to change the world.

With this practical sonic method—the technique of actually learning to intone the Divine Name for prayer—we can learn to utilize this amazing force together as a global community. When this occurs, the impossible becomes possible. Through this technique, we can make a quantum leap in consciousness. There is the potential that as we evolve as a species, we can gain extraordinary abilities once described by the ancients, such as telepathy or telekinesis, which will assist us even further in making positive planetary shifts.

Such potential abilities would occur only after we've achieved compassion on a global level, but as the Golden Rule points out, this is indeed a natural step in our conscious evolution.

I have no doubt that after reading this book, listening to the Instructional CD, and practicing the exercises that have enabled you to experience the Divine Name, you are different. Changed! Altered! You have evolved for the better because your energy and your awareness have shifted to a greater resonance with the Divine. This acceleration of consciousness will not only help you and those you're in a relationship with, but the planet itself.

I encourage each and every person reading this book and listening to the accompanying CD to utilize this profound technology of encoding this Divine sound with consciousness in order to make a difference for the planet. You don't need to wait for a global event in order to begin doing this—you can start right now.

Temple of Sacred Sound

To help initiate your work projecting sacred sound on a global level, I invite you to visit a Website I developed called **www .templeofsacredsound.org**, the world's first interactive cyberspace sacred-sound temple, which is accessible 24/7. At present, there are three separate toning chambers: "Om," "Ah," and "Hu." By visiting these, you can sound along with people throughout the world. In particular, the "Ah" chamber is highly recommended. Since "Ah" is one of the primary vowels of the Tetragrammaton, this chamber is extremely conducive to the intonation of the Divine Name. You can chant the Divine Name while here and know that you're sounding along with other beings throughout the planet.

Regardless of how you do this, I urge you to sound both individually and collectively for peace and harmony, and to utilize the Divine Name for this purpose.

It's Our Choice

As I wrote in the beginning of this book, the Divine Name has been the most powerful sound I've ever experienced. It continues to be so, many years later. And I continue to use it in my prayers and meditations on a regular basis.

I've been guided to share material for creating the Divine Name with you now, in order to facilitate both personal and planetary healing. I trust you will utilize this book, its accompanying CD, and the sound of the Divine Name in such a manner as to assist in bringing the energies of Divine Light and Love to this planet.

Take part in the process of Global Harmonization—of Tikkun Olam. Do it for yourself, your family, your friends, and all sentient beings on Earth. And most of all, do it for your children's children's children, so that ultimately generations from now, we will continue as a species, and will have created a better place for everyone. Remember: We heal the planet, we heal ourselves. We heal ourselves and we heal the planet! It's our choice.

Epilogue

The Aura-Imaging Phenomenon

I had just sent out the completed manuscript of *The Divine Name* to my editor. I was done with the book. It was the best I could do. I was content.

The next day I attended INATS, the International New Age Trade Show—a yearly event in Denver where authors, musicians, artisans, and many others speak, perform, or have booths displaying their works. Others, such as myself, do signings for those in attendance. The first day had been extremely busy for me, ending that night with my receiving two Visionary Awards, one for Best Meditational/Healing Music, for my CD *2012:*

Ascension Harmonics, and another for Best Website, which the Temple of Sacred Sound (**www.templeofsacredsound.org**) won. This was a great surprise to me, as well as quite an honor.

The following day my wife, Andi, and I arrived quite late at the show in order to spend a couple of hours looking around at what we had missed due to our busy schedule of activities the day before. As the show was just about to close down, I passed by a booth that had "aura photography."

The study of photographing the aura has been around since the 1930s, when two Russian scientists, Valentina and Semën Kirlian, accidentally discovered that by passing a slight electric current through a plate that contained living matter, they were able to observe some sort of color "discharge" that extended beyond the physical material—what has become known as the *aura* or the *electromagnetic field.* This work has progressed over many years until there are now cameras available that seem to be able to record different aura colors relating to the moods and other factors of the people who are being photographed. There's much skepticism about the validity of these cameras, although the photographs can be fascinating to look at.

At this booth, there was a monitor that displayed the real-time effects of people using the equipment. I was asked to sit down and try it. However, I was tired and ready to leave the show—not particularly interested in having my aura photographed. But for some reason, I was guided to sit down, and as an experiment, to see if any changes would occur in my aura while intoning the Divine Name. Apparently, when I did this, the results were quite startling to everyone around the booth, including the aura-camera operator. I had missed whatever had occurred, since my eyes were closed. I was asked to sound the Divine Name again. This time the results were recorded.

What I present now are photographs taken from a brief 20-second video made while I intoned the Divine Name.

It is not my purpose to validate aura photography or assign any particular meaning to what you'll see. I simply make these photos available for your perusal. Most aura photography shows one or two predominant colors swirling around a person. With these photos, there was an initial slight bluish purple before I began to vocalize the Divine Name. This bluish purple hue is not visible in the first of these black-and-white photos. However, as you'll see, in the pictures that follow the first, a pure white light begins to emerge and then envelop me.

No claims are made about what these pictures represent. I do find it most interesting that rather than the traditional change in the color of the photograph, which is usual when people try to affect their auras, these pictures demonstrate something quite different: As I started to sound the Divine Name, white light immediately began to manifest. I'd never seen that before. I don't believe anyone else had either.

I present these photos to you now with no agenda. They may well show one aspect of the power of the Divine Name to initiate light and love through sound. Or they may indicate something else. I trust you'll find them of interest.

1. Sitting quietly before sounding: attempting to get centered.

2. I begin to vocalize the Divine Name and white light starts to appear.

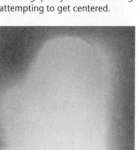
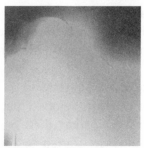

3. I continue to intone the Divine Name as the white light grows.

4. The more I sound, the more the white light continues to envelop me.

Afterword

Thank you so much for partaking in this journey of *The Divine Name.* I trust that you've found this book and the accompanying CD both educational and entertaining, and hopefully a bit enlightening. I believe that the information, techniques, and exercises you've encountered have the ability to positively change your life, and the world as well.

In truth, this is only the beginning. The more I continue to work with the Divine Name, the more extraordinary events and occurrences manifest as a result. Even the sounding of the Divine Name itself seems somehow to be fluid and otherworldly, changing in tone and texture, as it's needed.

I wish I'd been able to share *all* my experiences with the Divine Name. And I also wish I could provide explanations for these experiences. Perhaps that will be for another time and another book. Or perhaps it is to be revealed in workshops and the like. Regardless, it doesn't matter. There is much more. This is only the beginning.

For the moment, I simply want to honor you for your participation in this step-by-step process of vibratory activation using sacred sound. I have no doubt that by using the materials of *The Divine Name,* you have been changed and are different—in a positive way—and you will have created greater peace and harmony for yourself and for the planet.

May this book help the Divine Name be revived and remembered from generation to generation to generation.

Blessings of Love & Light Through Sound,
Jonathan Goldman

Frequently Asked Questions

1. With so many different religions and spiritual paths, how can there be just one Divine Name?

There are literally thousands, perhaps even millions, of different sacred names of God. Having been in this field for more than three decades, I've worked with many of these sacred names. They are all quite special and powerful. The Divine Name is composed entirely of vowel sounds, which are nondenominational and transcend individual religions and spiritual paths. When intoned properly, these vowels create the Tetragrammaton from the Abrahamic traditions. Thus, the Divine Name is both a universal sound and also the personal name of God.

With the Divine Name, I discovered a sound that utilizes all the vowels and brings the energy from the crown chakra down to the root chakra and then back up to the crown, going from spirit to matter and then back to spirit. It is a sound that resonates all our energy centers and unites us with the Divine. The fact that anyone can experience this resonance, regardless of his or her belief system, is just one aspect of the extraordinary power and majesty of the Divine Name.

2. Why is it so important to work with the accompanying Instructional CD in conjunction with the book?

As we've learned in these pages, the energy of sound is a multi-faceted phenomenon. It's not simply the sounds we create that enable the effect, but also the consciousness (what I refer to as *intent* or *prayer*) that is encoded upon the sound. Thus, simply mimicking the sounds I make may have some effect—as all self-created sound does—but it will not have the extraordinary effect that sounding the Divine Name does. This can only be achieved through working with the book and Instructional CD in combination.

3. Why has it taken so long for the Divine Name to emerge?

Many people have been taught that the Divine Name—or any name of God—should never be written or spoken. As we learned in our examination of the Old Testament, there is no edict against using the Divine Name. In fact, there is no edict against using any of the various names of God. However, there are those who have either not read these scriptures or have misinterpreted them. From my perspective, after extensive inner and outer examination of this topic, it seems appropriate to make this book and the CD available.

4. Is there a correct key, pitch, or note in which to sound the Divine Name?

No—there is no "correct" key, pitch, or note (they all mean basically the same thing). Any note is good as long as you feel comfortable and relaxed making the sound. The only "incorrect" note would be one where you experience strain or discomfort. In this case, simply try raising or lowering your voice until you find a pitch that is comfortable for you.

5. Are there any precautions you would recommend with regard to using the Divine Name?

Some may be concerned about the potential "inappropriate use" of the Divine Name. This simply cannot occur. There is a fail-safe mechanism built into it. To truly experience the power of the Divine Name, you need to be in a heartfelt vibration of appreciation, love, and gratitude. Among other things, this creates a powerful coherent field between your heart, your brain, and the external electromagnetic field of the planet. The Divine Name can't be effectively utilized when someone isn't manifesting positive feelings. Because of this, an individual who is feeling negative emotions would be denied the experience and the grandeur of sounding the Divine Name. At best, the improper application of such prayer would be totally ineffective. Thus, using the Divine Name as anything less than a heart-based phenomenon just doesn't work.

6. Is there more that I can do to study and experience the Divine Name?

First and foremost, the best thing you can do is to continue working with the Divine Name as presented in this book. You may find it helpful to reread the chapters and listen again to the Instructional CD—there's a lot of information and sound found within. The more you work with sound—particularly sacred sound—the more you'll be able to feel it resonating in your physical body, chakras, and energy field. Thus, it's necessary to continue practicing this vocalization to gain experience sounding the Divine Name.

Second, I present workshops on the Divine Name. This will give you the opportunity to experience sounding it with me. Many have found that such an initiatory experience is truly helpful. It's been suggested by Reb Zalman Schachter-Shalomi, considered one of the foremost Kabbalistic mystics of our times, that this is the best way to receive transmission of the Divine Name.

7. Can we really change the world with this sound?

All indications are positive. It's up to you and me! It's our choice now!

The Divine Name Instructional CD
Track Listing

Recorded Examples

1. Introduction

2. Pronouncing and Sounding the Vowels

3. Vowels as Mantra: Part I (One Breath for Each Vowel—Ascending Order) from Chapter 9

4. Vowels as Mantra: Part II (One Breath for Each Vowel—Descending Order) from Chapter 9

5. Vowels as Mantra: Part III (One Breath for All Chakras—Ascending Order) from Chapter 9

6. Vowels as Mantra: Part IV (One Breath for All Chakras—Descending Order) from Chapter 9

7. Intoning the Divine Name: Part I (Two Breaths for All Chakras—Descending and Ascending Order) from Chapter 10

8. Intoning the Divine Name: Part II (One Breath for All Chakras—Descending and Ascending Order) from Chapter 10

9. Intoning the Divine Name: Part III (Sounding the Divine Name) from Chapter 10

10. Conclusion

Recommended Resources

Resources from Jonathan Goldman

Books

Healing Sounds (Inner Traditions)
Shifting Frequencies (Light Technology)
Tantra of Sound (with Andi Goldman) (Hampton Roads)
The 7 Secrets of Sound Healing (Hay House)

Music

With over 25 CDs available, here is a selection that focuses on either sacred sounds, mantras, or the chakras:

Chakra Chants
Chakra Chants II
The Lost Chord
The Angel and the Goddess
Medicine Buddha
Ultimate Om
Holy Harmony
The Divine Name (with Gregg Braden)
Tantra of Sound Harmonizer (with Andi Goldman)
Crystal Bowls Chakra Chants (with Crystal Tones)
2012: Ascension Harmonics
2013: Ecstatic Sonics
Trance Tara
Sacred Gateways
Healing Sounds Instructional
Vocal Toning the Chakras

Resources from Others

There are myriad books and CDs that are relevant to the Divine Name and the field of sound. Here are some favorites:

Books on Sound

Music and Sound in the Healing Arts, by John Beaulieu (Station Hill)

The Healing Forces of Music, by Randall McClellan, Ph.D. (iUniverse)

Music: Physician for Times to Come, compiled by Don Campbell (Quest Books)

The Power of Sound, by Joshua Leeds (Healing Arts Press)

Toning: The Creative Power of the Voice, by Laurel Elizabeth Keyes (DeVorss & Company)

The Healing Power of the Human Voice, by James D'Angelo (Healing Arts Press)

The Mystery of the Seven Vowels, by Joscelyn Godwin (Phanes Press)

Following Sound into Silence, by Kailash (Hay House)

The Healing Power of Sound, by Mitchell L. Gaynor, M.D. (Shambhala)

The World Is Sound: Nada Brahma, by Joachim-Ernst Berendt (Destiny Books)

The Mysticism of Sound and Music, by Hazrat Inayat Khan (Shambhala)

Sound Medicine, by Wayne Perry (Career)

Words of Power, by Brian Crowley and Esther Crowley (Llewellyn)

Mantras: Words of Power, by Swami Sivananda Radha (Timeless)

The Yoga of Sound, by Russill Paul (New World Library)

Healing Mantras, by Thomas Ashley-Farrand (Wellspring/Ballantine)

Books on Kabbalah, Mysticism, and Prayer

The Secrets Doctrine of Kabbalah, by Leonora Leet (Inner Traditions)

The God Code, by Gregg Braden (Hay House)

The Isaiah Effect, by Gregg Braden (Three Rivers)

The Power of the Word, by Donald Tyson (Llewellyn)

Magic of the Ordinary, by Gershon Winkler (North Atlantic)

An Introduction to the Keys of Enoch, by J. J. Hurtak (Academy for Future Science)

Meditation and Kabbalah, by Aryeh Kaplan (Jason Aronson)

God Is a Verb, by David A. Cooper (Riverhead)

Wrapped in a Holy Flame, by Rabbi Zalman Schachter-Shalomi (Jossey-Bass)

The Prayer of the Kabbalist, by Yehuda Berg (Kabbalah)

Sefir Yetzirah, by Aryeh Kaplan (Weiser)

The Zohar, by Daniel C. Matt (Stanford University)

Jesus in the Lotus, by Russill Paul (New World Library)

Building Blocks of the Soul, by Matityahu Glazerson (Jason Aronson)

The Jew in the Lotus, by Rodger Kamenetz (HarperOne)

The Wisdom of the Hebrew Alphabet, by Michael L. Munk (Mesorah)

Music

Hearing Solar Winds—David Hykes

Tibetan Master Chants—Lama Tashi

Lightship—Tom Kenyon

Chants of the Hebrews—Gila Cadry

Heart of Perfect Wisdom—Robert Gass

Sacred Tibet—Gyume Monks

Chakra Healing Chants—Sophia

Spirit Come—Christian Bollmann

Fly, Fly My Sadness—Angelite & Huun-Huur Tu

Tibetan Chants for World Peace—Gyuto Monks

Angels' Waltz—Sada Sat Kaur

Overtones in Old European Cathedrals: Thoronet—Michael Vetter

Harmonic Divergence—Rollin Rachele

Kirtan—Jai Uttal

The Essence—Deva Premal

Sacred Feminine Voices of Bhutan—Bhutanese Nuns, with Raphael and Kutira

✦❈✦

For more information on my books, CDs, and other sonic tools for transformation, as well as on the therapeutic and transformational uses of sound and music, please contact:

Healing Sounds
800-246-9764 or 303-443-8181
www.healingsounds.com

For information on the Sound Healers Association, including material on finding and networking with sound healers, as well as many other resources, please contact:

Sound Healers Association
800-246-9764 or 303-443-8181
www.soundhealersassociation.org

To experience the Temple of Sacred Sound, the world's first interactive cyberspace sacred-toning temple, please visit:

www.templeofsacredsound.org

Acknowledgments

The Divine Name is the result of years of work and experience —of outer sound and inner listening. There are numerous people who have assisted and encouraged me in the creation of this book. To thank them all would be impossible, but here are a few:

To all the people at Hay House, including Louise Hay, Reid Tracy, Jill Kramer, Alex Freemon, Stacey Smith, Amy Gingery, Charles McStravick, Summer McStravick, Nick Welch, and all of the extraordinary beings who make this publishing house such a loving family.

To Sarah Benson and her husband, Donald Beaman. Sarah has left the earth to higher realms in order to continue her teaching. I give thanks to Don and Sarah for all the wisdom and love I received from you both and for having supplied the couch that I slept on when I first had that extraordinary dream that led to my discovery of the Divine Name. Indeed, the true sound of healing is love.

To Gregg Braden. I doubt that my work with the Divine Name, or any of the recordings or teachings on this subject, would have manifested without your friendship and support. It is rare to find such resonance in another human. Your wisdom and integrity are inspirational. I am grateful.

To all the people who have contributed to my work with sound, light, and love. They are too numerous to name now. Thank you for the teachings and initiations and experiences that have ultimately led to this book. In particular, though, I would like to cite the assistance of Rabbi Auri V. Ishi, who helped with our understanding of the Torah and gave me Smiha; to Makasha, who acted as a sounding board for me; to Reb Zalman Schachter-Shalomi, who gave me his blessings for this book and this work; to Alec Sims, whose thoughtful and insightful suggestions truly assisted my writing; and to Jim Wright, who provided synchronistic support when it was needed.

To all the people who have already received and experienced the Divine Name through workshops and other such teachings—your response has been an extraordinary source of encouragement that this was the correct path to take. To my beloved wife, Andi—you know I couldn't have created *The Divine Name* without you. You understand my work and my purpose. With your love and wisdom, you have helped me in ways far beyond just editing this book—we are partners together in all that we do. Mere words alone cannot articulate my thankfulness for your essence and for your being with me. You are my favorite psychotherapist and sound healer. And of course, you are my Angel of Love.

To my son, Joshua—you are awesome, compassionate, and wise; and certainly the best legacy I can imagine. Your evolution into manhood continues to provide inspiration and guidance for me, both as a father and as a friend.

To all the beings of light and love who work with and through me, I cannot express enough gratitude and appreciation for your help. Thank you for continuing to enable me to manifest this purpose. In particular, special thanks to Shamael, Angel of Sacred Sound; and to the Voice that continues to guide me. I trust this book will help revive the Divine Name and assist the planet!

About the Author

Jonathan Goldman is considered to be one of the founders of modern sound healing, pioneering the field for 30 years. An award-winning musician and writer, he is the author of several books and more than 25 CDs. His work combines the spiritual and scientific aspects of sound as a healing and transformational modality.

A former blues and rock musician and filmmaker, Jonathan had a transformational experience that changed his life course. In the 1980s, he founded both the Sound Healers Association (which he directs), dedicated to education and awareness of sound and music for healing; and Spirit Music (of which he is CEO), producing music for meditation, relaxation, and self-transformation. Jonathan received a master's degree from Lesley University researching the uses of sound and music for healing. He has worked with masters of sound from both the scientific and spiritual communities and has been initiated in many different traditions, including as a swami in the lineage of Swami Satyananda and as a rabbi in the tradition of Reb Shlomo Carlebach. He has been empowered by the Dalai Lama's Chant Master of the Drepung Loseling Monastery to teach Tibetan overtone chanting. In addition, he is a lecturing member of the International Society for Music and Medicine.

Jonathan's books include *The 7 Secrets of Sound Healing; Healing Sounds; Shifting Frequencies;* and *Tantra of Sound* (co-authored with his wife, Andi), which won the Visionary Award for Best Alternative Health Book. His cutting-edge, award-winning recordings include *Chakra Chants, 2012: Ascension Harmonics, The Lost Chord, The Divine Name* (with Gregg Braden), *Frequencies,* and *Reiki Chants.* Jonathan's *Ultimate Om* CD was named one of the Top 20 New Age CDs by *New Age Retailer.*

His CD collaboration with Tibetan Chant Master Lama Tashi, *Tibetan Master Chants,* was nominated for a Grammy Award for Best Traditional World Music.

An internationally acknowledged master teacher, Jonathan facilitates Healing Sounds seminars at universities, hospitals, holistic-health centers, and expos throughout the United States and Europe. He has appeared on national television and radio, including *Coast to Coast AM,* and has been featured in periodicals such as *USA Today* and *The New York Times.* His annual Healing Sounds Intensive program attracts participants from throughout the world.

For further information, please contact Jonathan's office:

Healing Sounds
P.O. Box 2240
Boulder, CO 80306
(800) 246-9764 or (303) 443-8181
Website: **www.healingsounds.com**
E-mail: info@healingsounds.com

Hay House Titles of Related Interest

YOU CAN HEAL YOUR LIFE, the movie, starring Louise L. Hay & Friends
(available as a 1-DVD program and an expanded 2-DVD set)
Watch the trailer at: **www.LouiseHayMovie.com**

THE SHIFT, the movie, starring Dr. Wayne W. Dyer
(available as a 1-DVD program and an expanded 2-DVD set)
Watch the trailer at: **www.DyerMovie.com**

❖❊❖

ASK THE KABALA ORACLE CARDS, by Deepak Chopra and Michael Zapolin,
with Alys B. Yablon

**THE BIOLOGY OF BELIEF: Unleashing the Power of Consciousness,
Matter & Miracles,** by Bruce H. Lipton, Ph.D.

FOLLOWING SOUND INTO SILENCE: Chanting Your Way Beyond Ego into Bliss,
by Kurt (Kailash) A. Bruder (book-with-CD)

THE GOD CODE: The Secret of Our Past, the Promise of Our Future,
by Gregg Braden

MESSAGES FROM WATER AND THE UNIVERSE,
by Masaru Emoto (available July 2010)

**THE MOSES CODE: The Most Powerful Manifestation
Tool in the History of the World,** by James F. Twyman

SOLOMON'S ANGELS, by Doreen Virtue

SOUND SPIRIT: Pathway to Faith, by Don Campbell (book-with-CD)

YOUR SOUL'S COMPASS: What Is Spiritual Guidance?
by Joan Borysenko, Ph.D., and Gordon Dveirin, Ed.D.

All of the above are available at your local bookstore,
or may be ordered by contacting Hay House (see next page).